"Filled with research-proven, practical sugg[...] [...]ing stress in teens, this insightful book can[...] and calm in the face of the daily challenges of life. This is a step-by-step guide with accessible practices as well as interesting proposals about intuition and relationships, offering new ways of strengthening your mind and improving your life. Dive in and feel the power of this approach!"

—**Daniel J. Siegel, MD**, *New York Times* bestselling
author of *Brainstorm* and *Mind*

"Less stress, less drama, more true friends! *Transforming Stress for Teens* provides the skills and knowledge teens need to take back their power, and experience both acceptance and understanding. Fit in, be loving, and be loved, yet remain uniquely and genuinely you! A must read."

—**Becky A. Bailey, PhD**, internationally acclaimed
author and speaker, and creator of the Conscious
Discipline system of self-regulation for parents,
teachers, and students

"Accessible and engaging, this book provides what today's teens need—practical tools to help them manage emotions, navigate their world with greater ease, and be more of who they truly are. It is a gem, and I will wholeheartedly recommend it to the teens and parents I work with."

—**Judy Grupenhoff, MS, MEd**, youth specialist at
Providence Behavioral Health Hospital

D0198352

WITHDRAWN
CEDAR MILL & BETHANY LIBRARIES

"*Transforming Stress for Teens* sets itself apart from the large number of available books and workbooks for adolescents on managing stress, by moving beyond simple discussions of relaxation and awareness strategies, and additionally explaining and emphasizing the key role that emotional experience and emotional regulation play in truly mastering stress in all aspects of life. I find this book to be unique among self-help books for adolescents in its discussion of fascinating (and important) topics such as coherence, the heart-brain connection, intuition, and communication in very clear language with great real-life examples. The authors do an exemplary job making the chapter topics interesting and relevant for teens in their day-to-day experience, and then provide tools and techniques that are time-efficient and easy to use."

> —**Timothy Culbert, MD, FAAP**, developmental/behavioral pediatrician and medical director of the Integrative Medicine Program at PrairieCare Medical Group in Minneapolis, MN

"It's a fact—teen life is stressful! It seems the pressure is always on to make (and keep) friends, make the grades, make the team, and, most importantly, make sure parents are pleased. Research indicates that adolescents who learn to identify and overcome everyday stressors now, are better able to navigate through tough situations, reduce stress, and remain resilient as adults. *Transforming Stress for Teens* is the perfect guide to help teens learn easy-to-use tools and techniques to beat stress and thrive for the rest of their lives."

> —**Susan Alford**, state director of South Carolina's Department of Social Services

"For the last several years at Olympia Sports Camp, we have taught the ideas and tools found in this book to thousands of youth to help them learn how to manage their emotions instead of just reacting to life situations. With *Transforming Stress for Teens*, teens can become the hero of their own journey by learning the qualities of their deeper hearts while on the path of discovering who they really are. I highly recommend this book."

> —**Dave Grace**, founder and director of Olympia Sports Camp in Ontario, Canada

"Young people today experience a high level of stress. This greatly affects their potential for optimal performance. I have found HeartMath® techniques to be both practical and simple for their day-to-day lives. I highly recommend this book to every young person in search of a technique for coping with stress."

> —**Jorge Calzadilla, MEd**, vice president of the Division of Public Service at Florida Atlantic University, former executive director of Clemson University's Youth Learning Institute (YLI), and board member of The Conservation Fund's National Forum on Children and Nature, Institute of HeartMath®, and the National Youth Advocate Program

"*Transforming Stress for Teens* is a wonderful resource of practical strategies and tools to help teens reduce their stress and build resilience. I love how each chapter reinforces the concepts and tools presented in previous chapters. The exercises are thoughtful, practical, easy to complete, and will help teens make healthier decisions with a renewed sense of hope and self-reliance. I am confident that thousands of teens will greatly benefit from the practical advice laid out in this book."

—**Jacqui Letran, NP**, teen confidence expert, speaker, and author of *I Would, but My Damn Mind Won't Let Me!* and *Five Simple Questions to Reclaim Your Happiness*

the *instant* help
solutions series

Young people today need mental health resources more than ever. That's why New Harbinger created the **Instant Help Solutions Series** especially for teens. Written by leading psychologists, physicians, and professionals, these evidence-based self-help books offer practical tips and strategies for dealing with a variety of mental health issues and life challenges teens face, such as depression, anxiety, bullying, eating disorders, trauma, and self-esteem problems.

Studies have shown that young people who learn healthy coping skills early on are better able to navigate problems later in life. Engaging and easy-to-use, these books provide teens with the tools they need to thrive—at home, at school, and on into adulthood.

This series is part of the **New Harbinger Instant Help Books** imprint, founded by renowned child psychologist Lawrence Shapiro. For a complete list of books in this series, visit newharbinger.com.

transforming stress for teens

the **heartmath** **solution** for **staying cool** under **pressure**

ROLLIN MᶜCRATY, PʜD
SARAH MOOR
JEFF GOELITZ
STEPHEN W. LANCE, MS

Instant Help Books
An Imprint of New Harbinger Publications, Inc.

Publisher's Note

This publication is designed to provide accurate and authoritative information in regard to the subject matter covered. It is sold with the understanding that the publisher is not engaged in rendering psychological, financial, legal, or other professional services. If expert assistance or counseling is needed, the services of a competent professional should be sought.

Distributed in Canada by Raincoast Books

Copyright © 2016 by Rollin McCraty, Stephen W. Lance, Jeff Goelitz,
      and Sarah Moor
      Instant Help Books
      An Imprint of New Harbinger Publications, Inc.
      5674 Shattuck Avenue
      Oakland, CA 94609
      www.newharbinger.com

Cover design by Amy Shoup

Acquired by Tesilya Hanauer

Edited by Jean Blomquist

All Rights Reserved

Library of Congress Cataloging-in-Publication Data on file

FSC
www.fsc.org
MIX
Paper from
responsible sources
FSC® C011935

18   17   16

10   9   8   7   6   5   4   3   2   1   First Printing

This book is dedicated to you, the teens who are looking for a clear way to find your own self-empowerment in today's fast-paced, stressed-out world. May you find the empowerment that comes from the alignment of your mind and emotions with your heart's intuition.

Contents

Foreword

If you are a teen or a helper for teens and have picked up this book, I applaud you. You are here seeking answers to address teen stress, and what you will find here will help you in ways you have probably never imagined. This stress solution only requires a little bit work of and commitment. These techniques and exercises are based on the hard science of our brains and bodies. They have helped other teens manage stress and find success. I know them to be truly effective because they have helped over a thousand teens in my programs.

Today's world is an increasingly stressful place for teens. Youth today are faced with immense and increasing stresses, including bullying, divorce, drugs, and even violence. The digital media world swamps us with information and can be like taking a bath in stress. Regardless of the form of stress we are facing, our brains react in a pattern that has been established over time. This book, with its Heartmath solution, offers a healthy alternative pattern to counter those established patterns and master stress.

I found HeartMath's solution to managing a stress-filled world when I had been working with extremely troubled teens, as well as high-level adolescent athletes, for about eight years. This introduction included HeartMath's techniques and its accompanying easy-to-use technology. I had never encountered a more scientifically sound yet simple way to manage stress. I began to experiment and discovered various ways to teach the information successfully to adolescents. Even the most resistant and stressed youth told me they could feel it working. In my programs, we have done this work with large groups of youth, individuals, and even families for the last eighteen years. All of this work has created the same result: mastery of one's internal world while navigating the rough seas of the adolescent stage of life.

Through the years I have seen many youth heal from various levels of stress, anxiety, and even trauma through the power in HeartMath's techniques. One particular young man comes to mind. He suffered from depression and struggled socially, his parents were divorced, and he managed stress poorly. When he completed our program he believed in the Quick Coherence technique so deeply that he went on to train his entire Post Wilderness Program therapeutic school's staff and all of the students there. He even presented on the original HeartMath book, *Transforming Stress*. HeartMath transformed his life and he carried it on to help others de-stress.

I have often wished that, during my time navigating the rough seas of my own teen years, I would have had these solutions. I was a teen with a divorced family, an angry father. All of the stresses of life built to the point of my needing relief. I was desperate for a way out but had no healthy solution, and I grasped for any way out I could find. Unhealthy endeavors became a short-term solution that led to more stressors and more alienation.

Do yourself, and the teens you care about, a favor and reach for this healthier, effective HeartMath solution!

—Steve Sawyer, LCSW CSAC
Chief Clinical Officer
New Vision Wilderness Therapy Programs

Introduction
Learning to Transform Stress

Imagine for a moment that you and a friend are drifting on a raft out in the ocean. Together you paddle for days and days in search of land. Finally, you're both so worn out that neither of you can lift the oars anymore. All hope of finding land is lost and you give up. You're lying on the bottom of the raft waiting to die. Then you sit up and look around—in the distance, you see what appears to be a patch of land. Hope! This one moment of hope renews your strength and vitality. You find hidden energy reserves and you begin to paddle vigorously to shore, whereas one minute before you were exhausted and felt like you were dying.

How does a feeling like hope bring vitality and renewed energy? How does it have the ability to completely change how a situation looks, from something that feels hopeless to one of possibilities? How does it motivate and inspire a person to take action and provide the necessary energy to do so? How does a feeling like hope transform stress?

This book will help answer those questions. A central message of this book is that there really is *hope* because there actually are solutions that can transform stress. You can learn not only to manage your stress, but even to prevent much of it before it happens.

More importantly, the techniques in this book will help you tap into the power of renewing emotions, such as hope, appreciation, joy, confidence, calm, and courage—the very things that can bring meaningful change to the day-to-day challenges in your life. Stress is rising among most teens in a very big way. In fact, according to a 2013 survey by the American Psychological Association, teens now rate themselves as having more stress than adults. It's time to *do* something about it and not just talk about it!

To enjoy life more, get along better with people, and accomplish things that are important to you, managing your stress is a must—otherwise, stress manages you. In this book, we'll help you learn to manage your stress by making your day-to-day life more like surfing—by *riding* the waves of emotion and daily challenges instead of letting the waves knock you over. We'll talk a lot about how you can ride those waves by being more responsible for your actions and reactions. This book, then, will show you how to manage your responses to daily stressors and challenges—and it may be a little different than what you've learned in the past. So keep reading!

The key to managing your stress is learning how to better handle how you respond to everyday situations. That's an aspect of maturing. Let's say, for instance, that when you were a very young child, you weren't allowed to go out into your yard by yourself. When you got a little older and your parents could see that you were being responsible by staying in the backyard, they let you go out alone. Your world grew a little more when they let you play in the front yard, too, when they were comfortable that you understood not to go near the road. Eventually, your world expanded further when you were responsible in crossing the street to get to a neighbor's house and coming home at the agreed-upon time. Being self-responsible, then, is a foundation of maturity. As you mature, your world opens up and includes more opportunities—as well as more stress.

The goal of this book is to help you transform your stress. The techniques you will learn have helped many teens and adults around the world greatly reduce their stress and be more of who they truly are. You'll read some of their stories in the pages ahead so you can see how others use the techniques and how those techniques have helped them.

You'll learn techniques to slow down your emotional reactions so old patterns of anger, anxiety, frustration, impatience, and fear stop having control over you. You'll open yourself to a whole new attitude and outlook toward situations, people, and maybe even life itself. Part of what makes the techniques and exercises introduced in this book so effective is that you don't have to stop what you're doing because you can use them anytime and anywhere—and no one will even know you're using them! You'll know it, though, because you'll feel a difference. You might find that people notice a difference in you, too. If you really give these techniques a try, we are confident you'll be able to better manage your day-to-day stress rather than it managing you. By the end of this book, you're going to know how to better handle challenging situations so you don't get walloped over the head by them. By the way, you will have these skills for the rest of your life. You'll be way ahead of most adults.

This book was cowritten by people from the HeartMath Institute in California and the Youth Learning Institute of Clemson

University in South Carolina. Both organizations have worked with thousands of teens, teachers, and parents for many years and have learned ways to help teens be happier, make better grades, handle tough situations, improve sports performance, make smarter decisions, get along better with others, and enjoy life more. In fact, a school partnering with the Clemson University Youth Learning Institute incorporated the tools and techniques found in this book as part of its programs.

We want you to get as much practical, everyday benefit as you can from this book. At the end of chapters 1 through 8, you'll find an action plan with some exercises to do. Do each one! Who knows? You might start noticing a difference—a little less stress can go a long way. Be sure to have some paper, a notebook, or a journal to jot things down as you read. You won't have to write a lot unless you would like to, but some notes along the way may be really helpful. Plus, when you write something down, you're more likely to remember it.

Just as you and your friend on the raft found renewed energy and vitality because of the hope you felt at the sight of land, you can also transform the stress of your everyday challenges and situations to that same feeling of renewal and vitality so you can be more of who you truly are. Let's begin!

chapter 1

Resilience
The Key to De-Stressing and Becoming the Real You

You're up to your ears in it. It's everywhere you go. It keeps you awake at night, and it really gets you when you're taking a test. It's big. It's small. Your friends have it, too. In fact, your family has it and so do your teachers. You feel like you're maxed out. What *it* is—is stress! Stress seems to be everywhere. Some or a lot of the time, you feel overwhelmed or bored in school, upset or angry about a relationship, pressure to fit in, fearful of a new situation, or worried about a situation at home.

But that's not all. When you feel stressed because you got angry or frustrated about something, words may fly out of your mouth—even to your friends—and those words may not be the greatest things to say. You feel disappointed because you can't be as good as people expect you to be and when you feel a lot of pressure, it's difficult to do well in school—or to do anything well.

It's not just your brain that can't think clearly when you're anxious or nervous. Your body feels it, too. Your shoulders become tight and rise. Your jaw tenses, and sometimes you grind your teeth. Not to mention your upset stomach, which feels like it's in knots when you experience the pressure of everything piling up. You toss and turn in bed because it's hard to sleep or you're so emotionally exhausted you sleep a lot. Even when you're just sitting still, your foot pulsates up and down like it's running a race. All those clenching, tight muscles and your racing foot are signs that your emotions are over-amped and out of control, which drains a lot of your energy.

On top of that, life isn't as enjoyable when you're worried, fearful, or bored. Ever notice that? When you're stressed, you're more irritable and cranky. Things just get under your skin and you are quicker to get angry or frustrated. Sometimes it makes you want to be alone and not do stuff you really like to do. Even hanging out with your friends isn't as much fun. It can feel like there's pressure coming at you from all directions all the time. Feeling stressed is not a pretty picture.

"I have anxiety nagging at me all the time. This voice inside me says that I should be doing better. I should be doing the right thing. It just takes over. And then, if I do something that I probably shouldn't have, I worry about it for a week to see if I will get busted by my dad or my teachers."

So what can you do about your day-to-day stress? Instead of feeling overwhelmed, what if there was a way to transform the stress in your life? What benefits might you gain if you transformed your stress? Let's take a look now at what that might mean for you.

Why Manage Stress?

At the heart of managing stress is how you *respond* to a situation. Challenging situations, big and small, are a part of life, no matter how old you are. It's *how* you handle those situations that counts.

Managing stress means learning to manage your emotions so you can deal with whatever comes your way with more balance, clarity, and self-assurance rather than with anger, impatience, frustration, or anxiety. When you can do this, you'll feel more confident, less doubtful or fearful, and you'll have less stress. When you get upset—and who doesn't?—it doesn't take as long to bounce back from disappointments and disagreements. You may find that you are more patient when stuff comes up, and you feel calmer and less rattled when doing things like taking a test or having an edgy conversation with someone.

Managing stress means managing your emotional reactions, which can make the difference between getting into a big argument and finding a way to work things out. When you de-stress, you have a better sense of what's important to you and what isn't worth your time or energy. You've got better things to do! With less stress, you can go about your day with fewer tight jaw muscles and knots in your stomach. Simply put, when you are able to manage your stress, you *feel* better and *do* better.

Here's what less stress means:

* being better able to sense what's really important to you

* bouncing back faster after challenging situations

* communicating and talking things through more effectively

* enjoying life more

* experiencing less boredom

* experiencing less drama

* feeling calmer and more confident

* handling situations better on the spot

* having greater ability to concentrate and stay focused

* having more patience

* making better decisions

* thinking more clearly

What would having less stress mean to you in your life? Take your time with this question. What would your day or even one situation look like, if you experienced less stress? What would you feel like if you had less stress? Take a moment and write your thoughts down in your notebook.

Now that you've thought a bit about how you would feel if you had less stress, how exactly can you experience less stress in your day-to-day life? As we've said, managing stress means managing your emotional reactions. That's not always as easy as it sounds. Building your resilience will help increase your ability to better handle all the daily stuff that comes your way and is an important key for transforming stress. HeartMath defines *resilience* as the capacity to prepare for, recover from, and adapt in the face of stress, challenge, or adversity. The techniques in this book will help you build resilience so you have greater ability to handle situations. We'll talk specifically about resilience a little later in this chapter, but right now, let's talk about *you* because less stress means more you—the *real* you!

The Real You Beneath the Stress

Obviously in a book about stress, we're going to talk a lot about it. But first, let's talk about the *real* you—the person you really are. The person, *you,* who is full of vitality, creativity, kindness, adventure, and fun. Okay, so that may feel a hundred miles away. We get that. You've got some tough stuff going on in your life that smothers all of who you really are—the best you, the resilient you. So before we talk about stress, let's talk about the real you.

Maybe it feels like you've been put down so many times that you've forgotten *you.* And for some of you reading this book, you may have indeed been belittled, put down, and let down for a long time. We want you to rediscover, or perhaps discover for the first time, what makes you come alive. We want you to know, feel, and live *all* of who you really are every day—or at least a whole lot more often. You have probably had pep talks like this before, but nothing ever came of it. This book introduces techniques that you can use anytime and anywhere to help you uncover, unleash, and unsmother *you*! Let's start with an exercise to help you uncover or rediscover the real you beneath all the stress.

Exercise: Finding the Real You

You'll need your notebook for this, so go ahead and get it out. We're going to ask you some questions to help you explore what the real you feels and looks like. You might want to find a quiet place so you won't have distractions or interruptions. This is your time. You might do a little now and come back to it again later. Or you might have some thoughts that come up at another time that you can add to your notebook when you get a chance.

Step 1: Take a few breaths that are a little slower and deeper than usual. This can help quiet mind chatter and scattered thoughts.

Step 2: Ask yourself: *Who am I underneath all the stress and day-to-day stuff that comes at me? What makes me come alive (that's legal and doesn't get me into trouble!)?*

It might be helpful to recall moments when you were "the best you," even if they were brief moments. Open your notebook and write down every uplifting, inspiring, renewing, fulfilling thing you know about yourself. As you think of other qualities, add them to your list. It's not that you have to have a long list. Even just a couple things can help you have a target to aim for. The target is simply *you* and not what others might say about you or think about you.

Here are some other questions you might ask yourself:

Did you feel creative, have lots of ideas, or maybe show a funny side of yourself and make people laugh?

Did you feel that you could accomplish things you set out to do and stick with it?

Did you have an "I can do this" attitude?

Were you courageous? Kind? Generous? Supportive?

Were you a team player? A leader?

What are positive things others have said about you that maybe
you brushed aside?

Step 3: Consider qualities you see in other people that you respect and
value:

Do they speak truthfully from their heart even when it's difficult to
do so?

Do they show respect?

Are they wise?

Do they have a good attitude?

Do they inspire and motivate others?

Are they honest?

What you see in them may be hidden qualities that you have.

Step 4: If you're having difficulty seeing anything worthwhile about yourself,
then *imagine* the person you would be if you were your very best. Not things
like being taller, shorter, skinnier, fatter, or smarter—it's not imagining the
person who has bigger muscles or who wears expensive designer clothes
and who has the latest smartphone.

More than likely, the qualities of the person you *imagine* yourself to be when
you are your best are really the qualities you truly possess—for example,
fun, creative, kind, honest, hardworking, adventuresome, love to learn (and it
doesn't have to be only learning things in your classes), a good friend, loyal,
and so on. Write these down in your notebook.

Step 5: Make a collage or draw pictures that represent the very *best* of
you—the you who is underneath all the stress. Have fun with this. You don't

have to be an artist. Stick figures are fine! Get out colored pencils to help make it fun. Some people make collages with lots of pictures that represent different parts of themselves—their silly and fun side, their strong side, or their wise side. You might find words or phrases in a magazine that describe you. Cut those out, too. Be sure to put the collage somewhere you can see it. That way, on days when nothing seems to be going right, you can remind yourself of who's really inside so you can find your way back to your real self.

Okay, now that you're getting to know who you really are, let's take a look at what gets in the way of you being the real you.

What Is Stress?

The word "stress" is used a lot in everyday language, but what does it really mean? We say things like, "School stresses me out" or "I get so stressed being around him." Stress, however, is not the "thing" that just happened or the situation on the outside—*stress* is the feeling or emotion you experience *inside* yourself *in response* to the "thing," that external event or situation. It's the emotion that makes you feel lousy, not the "thing" itself. The "thing" (event or situation) is called the *stressor*. You can think of the stressor as what "triggers" the feeling of being stressed.

Let's say, for instance, that you're wearing a favorite pair of jeans, and as you walk down the hall, they get caught on a locker door and rip—and it's a big rip. No repairing this one! You're fuming. We've all had stuff like that happen. Being mad is one of the feelings we experience when we say we are stressed. The stress is not caused by the ripped pants. The ripped pants are simply clothes and the locker door is simply a door. Stress is typically the feeling or emotion you experience in response to a situation or an interaction. In this case, the stress is the feeling of being mad that you experience about ripping your favorite pants.

Trying to sweep the stressful feelings under the rug doesn't work very well, especially in the long run. So let's turn the table on stress and look at it differently. We think you'll find that understanding stress from a different perspective will help you see that you can handle life's day-to-day situations more effectively.

The following are a few examples of feelings and emotions people often experience as stress. There are many more. In your notebook, write down any of these (or others you can think of) that you have experienced recently.

* anger

* anxiety

* bitterness

* boredom

* fear

* frustration

* helplessness

* hopelessness

* impatience

* numbness

"When I'm stressed, I get moody and angry."

* out of control

* overwhelmed

* pressure

* resentment

* sadness

* worry

But why do you experience stress? Could it be that stress tells you something important?

Stress: Warning Signs

The feelings of stress are actually warning signs that something is out of sync. If you ignore those signs, especially the emotional signs, you can get so used to the feeling of stress that stress becomes what you typically feel. But that does not mean stress is good for you. It just means that it is what feels familiar to you because you experience it often. When many people in a particular environment, like school, feel stressed much of the time, a climate of stress is created that seems almost natural. That can make it much more difficult for individuals to see their own stress clearly—unless they know how to.

As troublesome as stress is, it can actually be an opportunity for learning if you approach it positively and with an attitude like a detective. That means paying attention to the different "clues"—the signs of stress like anxiety, headaches, nausea, or becoming annoyed. Those signs alert you to the fact that you may be experiencing stress that you are not aware of. The signs of stress in your body can give you valuable clues about what kinds of things trigger stress for you and the unique ways that you respond. When you experience any of the signs of stress, it's a good time to practice one of the techniques in this book.

You can think of the list of emotions and feelings above as signs of stress. There are other signs of stress, too—mental, physical, and behavioral signs. The lists below give examples of each of these. Something that many people don't realize is that what is hiding beneath the mental, physical, and behavioral signs of stress is usually an emotional upset, such as the emotions listed above: frustration, sadness, anger.

As you read the following lists of mental, physical, and behavioral signs of stress, write down in your notebook any that apply to you. Add others that you come up with. Think of this as taking an inventory that reveals how your emotions can, in many different ways, affect your mind, body, and relationships. Signs are not bad. They are simply different ways people are affected by stress.

Mental Signs of Stress

* confusion

* difficulty focusing

* disorganization

* distraction

* failing grades

* forgetfulness

"My grades started slipping at the end of the year because I felt so much stress."

"I worry about everything and feel so confused."

"It's hard for me to focus on my homework."

"When I get overwhelmed, I just want to leave the world behind and go play Xbox."

15

* negative thoughts and attitudes

* never-ending worry

* poor decision making

* procrastination

* racing thoughts

Physical Signs of Stress

* body aches and pains

* body tension

* exhaustion, low energy, fatigue

* frequent colds and infections

* increased use of alcohol, drugs, or cigarettes

* nail biting, teeth grinding, hair twirling, pencil chewing, fidgeting

* not eating, eating too much, or eating things that aren't good for you

* sleeplessness

* upset stomach

Behavioral Signs of Stress

* arguments

* difficulty talking with others

"I can't sleep and I stop eating when I'm stressed."

"I get acne and blemishes when I feel a lot of stress."

"I have mini panic attacks and my throat feels tight."

"I feel like I have a heavy weight on my shoulders."

* dramatizing situations

* fighting/bullying

* frequent absences from school

* giving in to peer pressure

* irritation and annoyance with people

* lost friendships

* withdrawal from friends and family

"Family drama! We end up arguing all the time."

"There's so much pressure to do drugs and have sex that I withdraw, and then I feel lonely."

By paying attention to the signs of stress, you can know when something is out of balance in your life. And when you know that something is out of balance, you can find ways to decrease stress and get your life back in balance. You can get back to being the real you.

Resilience and Your Inner Battery

As we mentioned above, resilience plays a very important role in your ability to manage stress. Understanding how to build your resilience can help you reduce your stress. Remember that resilience is the capacity to prepare for, recover from, and adapt in the face of stress, challenge, or adversity. To understand how resilience applies to reducing your stress, think of your resilience as how much energy you have stored in your inner battery. Although you don't have an actual battery inside you like your cell phone does, your body works as though it has an inner battery. Just like your cell phone stores energy so you can talk and text, your body also stores energy.

The amount of energy you have in your inner battery affects you physically, mentally, and emotionally. After all, your body turns the food you eat into energy, the very energy that gives you the ability to do all the things you do throughout the day. You need physical energy to walk, climb stairs, carry your backpack, work out, play sports, and dance. You need mental energy to be able to focus and concentrate, think clearly, know what you want to say to someone, and remember things you have learned when taking a test. You also need emotional energy because it motivates and inspires you and makes life interesting and meaningful. Emotional energy is also what connects you to others, gives you the courage to do the right thing, helps you appreciate your successes, and enables you to be kind and caring. It gives you a deeper sense of purpose. Without emotions, you would be like a robot.

Here is a key to resilience that we want you to remember: When your inner battery has more energy stored in it, it means you're more resilient and better able to handle whatever comes up during the day. It's an inner energy that's available so you can bounce back faster when you get knocked off your feet and be better prepared to handle daily stuff—big or small. On the other hand, when your inner battery is low, you have less energy—physical, mental, and emotional—which makes it more difficult to be in charge of how you *respond* in situations. When your battery is drained, you may find things get under your skin more easily and you become upset more quickly. You may blurt out things or do things that later you wish you hadn't. It's more difficult to think clearly and make good decisions, which can make it nearly impossible to handle any situation well.

For example, can you think of someone who knows how to push your buttons, someone who knows just the right thing to say or do to upset you? You get mad or irritated and mumble to yourself about what the person has said or done. Who or what irritates, angers, or frustrates you? For many people, it's either someone they love and care about or it's a situation they can't control. Some people are more likely to fly off the handle when they feel bad physically, such as when they're sick or when they're feeling anxious. Other people hang on to anger from past situations and blow a fuse if someone looks at them the wrong way. For people who are impatient, situations that cause delays, such as a slow line at the drive-through window or a traffic jam, can quickly cause anger. Tempers flare at the smallest things. All of these—the people, places, and issues outside of you that push your buttons—your stressors—can quickly drain your resilience, which then can make it even more difficult to "take charge" of how you respond.

Now here's something interesting that most people don't fully understand or appreciate—it's something that can put you in the driver's seat rather than throw you under the stress bus: *emotions have a powerful effect on your inner battery and your resilience.* Some emotions, the lousy-feeling ones, drain your battery and your resilience, while other emotions, the ones that feel good, recharge it. This is very important because when you don't have much energy in your inner battery, meaning your resilience is low, it's much more difficult to be your best no matter what you're doing. When your inner battery is drained, it is more difficult to handle situations you may face—like trying to concentrate when you're taking a test. It's more difficult to respond appropriately rather than simply react to a situation. The lack of understanding of how to manage emotions is one of the main causes of today's stress epidemic. People believe that the thinking mind rules. But more often than not, it's our *emotions* that determine our choices and behaviors.

Recall a time when you were angry, overwhelmed, anxious, scared, frustrated, or irritated. (We call these types of emotions *depleting emotions* because they deplete or drain your energy.) You might have noticed that your heart raced and your body was tense. You weren't just imagining it. That's what was actually happening in your body. Experiencing strong depleting emotions like the ones mentioned above is like flooring the gas pedal of a car, resulting in a rapid emotional energy burn.

Some depleting emotions run quietly in the background, and you may not even notice them at first. These "quieter" depleting emotions drain your inner battery, too, but it tends to be a slow drain. Every small depleting emotion, even the ones you say are "no big deal"—like feeling worried, sad, bored, or lonely or when you withdraw from the world around you—drains your battery, and these small depleting emotions add up, big time. You accumulate stress when you carry around depleting emotions without resolving them. Depleting emotions aren't bad or wrong. They're just letting you know something is out of balance. So it's very important to stop energy drains, even the quiet ones. By stopping them, you not only minimize the energy drain, but you also put the brakes on stress. This means you have a smoother rhythm and pace throughout the day because you can handle things that come up in better ways.

The trigger feeling often starts with a stabbing feeling of anger, insecurity, or frustration. It's only human to have these feelings. Again, the feelings aren't bad. It's what you do with them that matters. So let's say that a classmate says something that angers you like, "You're really stupid." You feel yourself boiling over inside. If you let the anger take over, it can run freely and flood your thoughts and then affect your actions and decisions in such a way that you end up getting into a fight. If you let an emotion such as anger or irritation build, you can end up even more irritated or angry, which drains huge amounts of energy. When you allow moans and groans to go unattended with thoughts like *It's so unfair* or *That's just the way it is* along with feelings of blame, resignation, and frustration, your inner battery will be zapped.

On the other hand, feeling calm, enthusiastic, hopeful, and appreciative, for example, not only feels good, but also recharges your inner battery. (We call emotions like these *renewing emotions* because they renew or recharge your energy.) In the next chapter, we'll talk more about how that works and how to recharge your battery. We'll show you how to put renewing emotions to work for you. But before we do that, let's look more closely at *your* energy drains. Then we'll introduce a technique to help you prevent your energy from being drained.

The first step is to identify stressors—what drains your energy—and how they make you feel. Let's face it though. Most people have difficulty acknowledging their feelings and may fear that others will judge them if they talk about emotions. If you're like most teens, or people of any age for that matter, you don't like to admit you're hurting or feeling bad, that your emotions are running you ragged, or that you feel a slow burn inside. You'd rather ignore such feelings or take them out on others. It's not "cool" to appear "uncool." But when these energy-draining emotions are not identified and handled effectively, stress builds and you may blow up, hide under the covers, or freeze like a deer staring into headlights. As a result, your enjoyment of life diminishes and "being your best" is next to impossible.

Identifying your stressors is a very important step, so don't skip over the following exercise! It will help you better see what triggers stress for you. You'll need your notebook or journal for this exercise. Find a quiet place that is free of distractions and take your time doing it.

Exercise: What Drains Your Battery?

Part 1: Identify Your Stressors

Step 1: Listed below are things that teens commonly report as stressing them out. In your notebook, write down any that are stressors for you. You may think of others not on the list. Write those down, too.

- body image/weight

- college application process

- deadlines

- family conflict

- grades

- health problems—family or personal

- homework

- lack of sleep

- money problems

- new neighborhood or school

- parents' expectations

- part-time job

- pressure to have sex

- pressure to use drugs and alcohol

- relationship breakups

- sense of not belonging, feeling left out

- target of teasing, bullying, or dissing

- technology not working

- time pressure

- tryouts for activities like a sports team or drama club

- violent situations

That's quite a list of potential stressors, and you may have thought of others. They are the things that keep you from being all of who you really are.

Step 2: Look at each stressor you wrote down and rate it as to how much energy it drains from you, using this scale:

1 = slight energy drain

2 = medium energy drain

3 = big energy drain

Let's use homework as an example of how to do the exercise: If you feel a little stress about your homework, rate it as 1 (slight energy drain). If you experience medium stress about homework, rate it as 2 (medium energy drain). If you experience a lot of stress, rate it as 3 (you guessed it—a big energy drain).

For each one you rated as 1, 2, or 3, ask yourself how often you experience that energy drain. For any that you experience often, it's probably a major source of your stress and a big energy drain.

Part 2

We want you to do one more thing with your list. For each of the stressors, write down a word or two that describes how that stressor makes you feel. For example, do you feel anxious, overwhelmed, bored, angry, sad, worried, scared, pressured, frustrated, or impatient?

Take your time and think how each stressor affects your inner battery and resilience. This exercise will let you know what stressors are draining your energy. After all, before you can stop what drains your energy, you have to know what's causing it.

"I really found Heart-Focused Breathing helped me a lot with emotions, my relationships with my friends and family, and just in everyday life, especially when I'm stressed out."

The good news is—and it's *really* good news—that although you may not be able to change your stressors, you can learn to change how you respond to them. It all begins with *you* taking charge of your emotions and how you respond in situations. That puts you in the driver's seat. We'll now introduce a breathing technique that will help you do just that.

Heart-Focused Breathing Technique

There are many different types of breathing techniques, such as those used in martial arts and yoga. Each breathing technique has a purpose. You can think of Heart-Focused Breathing as a technique to stop your reaction to a stressor in the moment, which in turn stops the drain on your inner battery. It also creates an emotional pause so you don't react automatically. You can use this technique anytime, anywhere to help you handle challenging situations. When you do Heart-Focused Breathing, you put your attention around your heart area. This helps you refocus and

"I used Heart-Focused Breathing when I was in an embarrassing moment. I calmed down and then I handled the situation calmly."

feel calmer. Heart-Focused Breathing is simple, but it can pack a punch! As simple as it is, it takes practice to get all the benefits.

First, we'll introduce the technique. Then we'll give you some helpful tips about how to do it. And finally, you'll have a chance to practice the technique.

Technique: Heart-Focused Breathing

Focus your attention in the area of the heart. Imagine your breath is flowing in and out of your heart or chest area, breathing a little slower and deeper than usual.

Here are a few helpful tips to get the most out of Heart-Focused Breathing:

* Don't hold your breath. Be sure to breathe a little slower and deeper than usual. (For example, try to inhale for five seconds, exhale for five seconds.) Find an even, steady rhythm that is comfortable to you.

* If you find it awkward to shift your attention to the area around your heart, first focus on your left big

toe, wiggle it, and see how it feels and how easy it is to direct your attention. Now, shift your focus to the area around your heart or chest area. You can pretend to breathe through your heart or hold your hand over your heart to help focus your attention in this area. Keep your focus there for ten seconds or more. Your mind will probably begin to wander and when it does, refocus your attention on the area around your heart.

* Stay focused on your breathing, and be sure you're not checking text messages while you're doing it.

* You might find that it's helpful to close your eyes to shut out visual distractions, but as you get used to doing it, practice with your eyes open. This is very important because you want to be able to do Heart-Focused Breathing wherever you are, and most of the time, closing your eyes won't be appropriate. This is an on-the-go tool!

* Make a genuine effort when doing this technique. Otherwise, it won't work as well.

* If you call it by its name, Heart-Focused Breathing, you'll remember the two parts: heart focus and heart breathing.

Now, try Heart-Focused Breathing for one to two minutes: *Focus your attention in the area of the heart. Imagine your breath is flowing in and out of your heart or chest area, breathing a little slower and deeper than usual.*

Suggestion: Inhale five seconds, exhale five seconds (or whatever rhythm is comfortable).

After practicing the technique, do you feel calmer and more balanced? Do you have less mind chatter and feel less distracted? Is your body less tense and have your shoulders dropped? What else do you notice? Write down in your notebook anything you noticed or experienced.

When you practice Heart-Focused Breathing, you may not always feel like much is happening or that it's really making a difference. But it is. It all adds up! So use it even when you don't feel any stress—and especially use it when stressors trigger you. That's when it can make a big difference.

If you practice Heart-Focused Breathing throughout the day, you will find that it becomes more comfortable and natural. Then, when you really need it in a stressful moment, it will be easier to do. Although it's a simple technique, Heart-Focused Breathing can be more challenging to use when you're triggered unless you practice it when you don't need it. So practice it a lot and try to make it a new habit. As one person said, "I'm breathing all day anyway, so I'll make it Heart-Focused Breathing."

Heart-Focused Breathing can be done anytime, anywhere. It truly can be done "on the go." Practice Heart-Focused Breathing in everyday situations such as these:

* before doing homework

* on the way to school or work

* before and while taking a test

* when someone says or does something that irritates you

* before and during sports activities, or when the ref makes a bad call

* when you feel overwhelmed by homework or anything else

* when you feel fearful

* while walking across campus

* when waiting in line

* when you read something on social media that makes you mad

* when you feel pressure from parents, teachers, or even your peers

* while driving

Heart-Focused Breathing will not make miracles happen, but it can lower your stress levels in a big way. Heart-Focused Breathing, however, will work *only* if you use it. That's the only way you will get the benefits that thousands of other teens and adults report.

"When I do the breathing, I can think more clearly about what I'm doing in a situation rather than just reacting right away."

Now that you've learned the technique, it's time to put it to practice for a couple of days. It's also important to pay attention to what triggers stress for you and how you feel in those moments.

We've discussed in this chapter the importance of understanding that stress is how you feel, not the thing that happened.

And that's good because most of the time you can't change other people or fix situations, but you can learn how to handle whatever comes up. Handling your emotional reactions in day-to-day situations and challenges more effectively means less stress. Heart-Focused Breathing is the first step in stopping energy drains and those automatic reactions.

In the next chapter, we're going to show you how to quickly recharge your battery. We'll also talk about other ways that having a fully charged inner battery is important and beneficial.

Before going on to the next chapter, however, do the following action plan for the next two or three days or longer. There's no need to rush to the next chapter. If you want to manage your stress, the practices in the action plan *are a must*. Do them every day, wherever you are, whatever you are doing—and no one will even know you're doing them.

Your Stress-Bustin', Resilience-Boostin', On-the-Go Action Plan

1. Each day notice when you're draining your inner battery. Don't leave out the little energy drains! Describe in a word or two how each makes you feel. For example, "I feel hurt because a kid just dissed me. It makes me feel bad about myself, and I want to crawl in a shell and hide. In fact, I feel embarrassed. I have a test in an hour, and I know I'm not going to do well because this has really upset me and I can't be at my best." Take your time and write down what drains your energy so you can get a full picture.

2. Practice Heart-Focused Breathing several times every day. Practice it when you don't need it and also when you are triggered and feel an energy drain. What do you notice when you do Heart-Focused Breathing?

3. Identify one situation that triggers you and commit yourself to "take it on." Perhaps it's feeling frustration when you have to wait in the lunch line or annoyance because your brother or sister keeps wearing your clothes. Don't start with your biggest one. Each time you are triggered, practice Heart-Focused Breathing until you feel calmer and more balanced. What do you notice when you do it?

   Starting with a smaller goal gives you practice. You might think of it as building your resilience muscle. After all, most people don't walk into the weight room and start lifting two hundred pounds. It takes effort, focus, and practice to gain the ability to lift more weight or, in the case of managing stress, to gain the ability to feel calm or balanced.

chapter 2

Your Heart and Brain
The Power of Working Together

Now we're going to give you the inside scoop on managing your emotions, and how the heart and brain talk to each other! It's really important stuff to understand if you genuinely want less stress around challenging situations and more fun in your life. Research has shown that getting the heart and brain in sync can lead to better decision making—and even better test scores.

Some of what we will talk about may not be in your science book (at least not yet), but it's important for transforming your stress. As you read, try to relate what we talk about to your day-to-day life. That's what really counts because it will help make a difference for you in managing your stress.

The Heart-Brain Connection

So why are we talking about your heart in a book that aims to reduce your stress? Scientists have discovered that your heart actually has its own little brain, which neurocardiologists (specialists who study how the heart and brain work together) call the *heart-brain*. The heart-brain is not as complex as the brain in your head, but, like the brain in your head, it has lots of neurons, ganglia, and neurotransmitters, and it produces hormones. It also has the ability to sense all kinds of things going on in your body, and it performs other functions that also go on in the brain.

What's fascinating is that your heart and brain actually "talk" to each other all the time. It's like a two-way street between the brain in your head and the brain in your heart. The communication "street" between your heart and brain is called the *autonomic nervous system*, or ANS for short. The ANS, which has two branches, not only carries messages between your heart and brain, but it also regulates over 90 percent of all the things that happen automatically in your body—things like breathing, digestion, immune system function, and much more. Surprisingly, your heart sends more information to your brain than your brain sends to your heart! It's something most people are not aware of. Even many doctors are surprised when they hear that the heart sends lots of information to the brain. New research on optimal performance clearly shows that the quality of the signals sent by the heart has a powerful effect on the quality of that communication and whether our brain functions well or not.

We're going to show you how you can improve the communication between your heart and brain, which in turn can enhance your ability to think clearly and respond to challenges (life's day-to-day stuff) in a more intelligent way. We'll also teach you a new technique—the Quick Coherence technique—that will help you do just that.

Heart Rhythms

It has been known for a long time that your emotions affect your heart, specifically what are called your *heart rhythms*. Heart rhythms reflect the natural speeding up and slowing down of individual heartbeats. A look at heart rhythms shows if the speeding up and slowing down is happening in a "smooth" way or if it's chaotic.

Research at the HeartMath Institute Research Center shows that depleting emotions such as frustration, anger, anxiety, impatience, fear, and sadness—the ones that drain your inner battery, make you feel lousy, and show up when you're stressed—create a chaotic heart rhythm pattern. That chaotic signal goes straight to your brain and prevents the smart-thinking part of your brain from...well...being smart! People even say, "I'm so mad, I can't think straight!" And indeed that's the case. The chaotic signals also affect the part of your brain that has to do with self-regulation, which can contribute to making it difficult to handle situations effectively when you're upset about something.

On the other hand, emotions that feel good to you and recharge your inner battery—renewing emotions such as kindness, care, courage, appreciation, joy, and patience—create a smooth and ordered heart rhythm pattern. You feel more balanced, think more clearly, and have greater ability to handle stressful situations with a lot less emotional drama.

To illustrate the effect emotions have on your heart rhythms, take a look at the graphs below. These are graphs of the heart rhythms of someone who was hooked up to equipment that measures these rhythms. The graphs were taken just moments apart, but they look very different, right? What do you see in those graphs? Based on what we just said about emotions creating different heart rhythm patterns, in which graph do you think the person was feeling frustrated? In which one do you think the person was feeling appreciation?

Emotions and Heart Rhythms

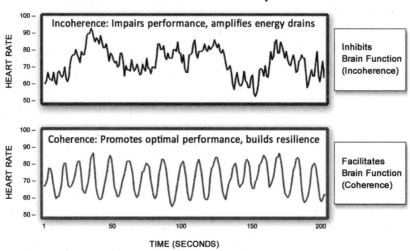

If you said that the top graph shows the heart rhythms when the person was feeling frustrated, you are absolutely correct. Doesn't it look like the way frustration feels? The chaotic pattern is what scientists call an *incoherent heart rhythm*. It looks like static!

The bottom graph shows the heart rhythms when the person was feeling appreciation. It looks like smooth, rolling hills and valleys. Just by looking at it, doesn't it give you more of a "smoother," calmer feeling? Scientists call this a *coherent heart rhythm*. So why is this important?

It's important because the pattern of your heart rhythms indicates the quality of the signals traveling between your heart and brain through the wires (the neural circuitry) of your autonomic nervous system—that two-way street that we talked about earlier. These signals can affect how well your brain works—or doesn't work. When you are mad, anxious, or worried, for example, your heart rhythm pattern looks like the top graph: herky-jerky and chaotic. That herky-jerky pattern impacts your brain. You can think of it like static in your brain, creating foggy thinking. It also means you may blurt out something because you're mad, but that you may later regret saying. The technical term for this is called *cortical inhibition.* It simply means that the cortex, which is the thinking part of your brain, is offline.

A good example of cortical inhibition is when you feel nervous or anxious taking a test. If you've ever had that happen, wasn't it difficult to think clearly? Once the test was over you may have said to yourself, *I can't believe I forgot that and I marked the wrong answer!* Or, in another situation, have you ever been so angry or overwhelmed that you couldn't think straight and nasty or hurtful words just flew out of your mouth? It feels that way because it *is* that way. Your brain can't think as clearly, and you can end up doing and saying things that you later regret or that even get you into trouble. Said more plainly, stress can make you say or do stupid things! Then you have to expend energy to "clean up" the mess you just made, which drains your resilience.

One student said, "It's hard for me to perform well at anything when I'm overly anxious. When I learned to manage my emotions, I performed better overall in my schoolwork and got along better with other people. It's almost impossible to understand information when I'm too anxious or overwhelmed."

If, however, you feel more patience, confidence, appreciation, courage, enthusiasm, care, or happiness, for example, your heart rhythms become smoother and more coherent. Naturally, your brain will then function better and you will make better decisions. When your heart and brain are in sync, that creates what scientists call *cortical facilitation*. That means the part of your brain that does the thinking and analyzing—the cortex—is functioning optimally. These signals are also sent to your entire body, which helps your glands and organs work together more efficiently and effectively. You even have better coordination and faster reaction times, which is why being "in sync" is so important in sports.

So, how do you get your heart and brain in sync? How do you develop those coherent heart rhythms? Let's take a closer look now at how to get your heart and brain to work together.

Coherence: Heart and Brain Working Together

Coherence is an important term that describes when things work together efficiently or perform optimally. Coherence, as discussed above, is when your heart and brain work together and are in sync. As a result, depleting emotions don't determine how you handle a situation. Coherence isn't only about heart rhythms. Think for a moment about a flock of birds that are flying together in formation, for example. Even though there may be hundreds or even thousands of them, they move together almost as if they were one organism. We could say they fly in a "coherent" way. Can you imagine what it would be like if a flock of birds didn't fly together as though they were one? They would be bumping into one another, and they probably would not get where they are going very efficiently. Most likely, they would have a lot of feathers missing, too!

Like a flock of birds, a soccer or football team needs to work or move together in a coherent way to get the ball down the field to set up for a chance to score. A group project goes more smoothly when each person does his or her part to get it done.

Another example of coherence is a sentence where all of the words come together so that they make sense. If you have to give a presentation to your class, you'll need to talk coherently if you want to get a good grade. You want to talk intelligently about your topic. However, if you're really nervous about talking in front of people—which is true for many people, adults included—try as you might, the words get tangled up on your tongue and they just won't come out in a way that makes sense. That increases your anxiety and you get more tongue-tied. Your words likely will form incoherent sentences. Have you ever had that happen to you? You may have even said to yourself that your brain was offline—and sure enough, it was. Feeling anxious and nervous creates incoherent heart rhythms, and those chaotic signals get sent to your brain!

But it's not only your brain that is affected when you feel anxious, nervous, or overwhelmed and your heart rhythms become incoherent—your whole body is stressed, too. You're draining your energy because the signals in your nervous system are out of sync. Those feelings also make it more difficult to be in charge of how you respond in a situation. So, how do you stop the stressful emotions that keep you out of sync?

It begins by realizing and understanding that you can put the brakes on stressful feelings. Then it takes committing and remembering to "take charge" of how you respond along with getting and staying coherent more often. Lots of research shows that using the techniques in this book to help you self-regulate and to self-generate healthy, renewing emotions can lead to improvements like these:

* better communication

* better decision making

* better feeling overall

* better sports performance

* greater ability to focus

* greater ability to stay calm in the heat of the moment

* higher test scores and better grades

* improved memory

* improved reaction times and coordination

* increased calm and balance

* increased self-confidence

* less boredom

* less reactiveness

* lower levels of stress hormones

* more creativity

* more flexibility in the way you think

As we said earlier, renewing emotions naturally create more coherent or smooth heart rhythms. *Renewing emotions* are the ones that feel good, such as joy, enthusiasm, appreciation, care, peace, love, kindness, or courage. However, and this is important, the power of a renewing emotion comes not simply from *thinking* about it but from *feeling* or *experiencing* it. Let's take a closer look at what we mean by that.

Usually, with a renewing emotion, something happens and it makes you feel good inside. For example, you buy a new outfit and wearing it makes you feel confident. Or you come home and your dog greets you, slobbers all over your face, and wants to play—and you feel a lot of love for him. Or perhaps you do well on a test, make a sports team, or a friend helps you with a project, and you feel happy, proud, or appreciative. These are all examples of things happening "outside" that make you feel good inside.

It's important to know, though, that you don't have to rely on something happening outside to make you feel good inside—and we're going to show you how to do this. Although it's an important life skill, it's something that most people are not taught how to do. Because your heart affects your brain—remember that two-way street between your heart and your brain—and your brain strongly affects your body, in order to stop stress reactions in their tracks, you need to shift your heart rhythms from an incoherent, jagged pattern to one that is ordered and coherent. How do you do this? You shift from experiencing a *depleting* emotion to experiencing a *renewing* one.

To help you learn how to do this, recall a time when you were doing something that you really enjoyed or that was meaningful to you. Perhaps you felt *happy* because you scored a goal, or maybe you experienced a feeling of *accomplishment* or *satisfaction* for doing well on a test or finishing a project. Perhaps a friend, your sibling, or someone else did something nice and unexpected for you, which you really *appreciated*. Or it might have been the feeling of *love* or *care* you had for your dog or cat, or feeling *peaceful, calm,* or *content* when you were outside in a park or in nature.

Take a few moments to think about this. Then, in your notebook, make a list of situations, places, or events when you have experienced a renewing emotion. See if you can also name the emotion or feeling you experienced. Writing them down can help anchor them in your memory, and you are more likely to remember them when you are stressed out. Here are some examples:

Situation, Place, Event	Renewing Emotion
Playing with my dog	Happiness, love
Getting a good test score	Satisfaction, confidence
Hanging out with my best friend	Appreciation, fun
Being out in nature	Calm, peaceful
Listening to music I like	Content, happy, inspired
Learning that a test was postponed until next week	Relief
Having someone stand up for you	Safe, accepted, appreciated

Each of the renewing emotions in the examples above helps create coherence. Let's put one of those renewing emotions that you identified and wrote in your notebook to work for you right now in the Quick Coherence technique.

Quick Coherence Technique

The Quick Coherence technique builds on Heart-Focused Breathing, which you learned in chapter 1. In addition to breathing, you reexperience or relive one of the renewing emotions you wrote down on your list. For example, let's say you feel love when your dog greets you after school. If you're at school, obviously your dog can't be there with you. But you know the feeling of love for your dog. So even though your dog isn't there with you, go ahead and feel that feeling of love, just like you do when he greets you when you come home.

Quick Coherence is a great name for this technique because, by practicing it, you can quickly reduce your stress, stop energy drains, and get more coherent. Your heart rhythms also become coherent—your heart and brain are in sync. The Quick Coherence technique enables you to *act* from your heart rather than *react* from unmanaged emotions, which is key to managing stress.

"I was feeling anxious before my math test. I wanted to feel calm so I did Quick Coherence and did the best I could to feel the calm feeling while I did the breathing. I remembered how I feel calm when I listen to quiet music, so I tried to experience that calm feeling again before the test. It took about three minutes to really feel calmer, but I kept trying and it worked."

Technique: Quick Coherence

Step 1: *Focus your attention in the area of the heart. Breathing a little slower and deeper than usual, imagine your breath is flowing in and out of your heart or chest area. Do this for one minute or more.*

Step 2: *Now, make a sincere attempt to experience a renewing emotion, such as appreciation or care for someone or something in your life. Do this for one minute or more.*

Here are a few helpful tips to get the most out of the Quick Coherence technique.

* Inhale for five seconds, and exhale for five seconds (or whatever rhythm is comfortable for you).

* Try to reexperience the feeling you have for someone you love—a person, a pet, a special place—or for an accomplishment. Or, focus on a feeling of calm or ease.

* Try to genuinely *experience* the renewing emotion and not just think about the thing that makes you feel good.

* Practice even when you don't feel you need it so it becomes more familiar. Don't give up trying it if you don't notice anything the first time you do it or if it feels a little awkward. You'll get the hang of it.

Now try the Quick Coherence technique for one to two minutes, following steps 1 and 2 above.

After trying the Quick Coherence technique, notice if you feel any calmer. What else do you notice? Do you have less mind chatter? Do you feel less distracted and more focused? Is your body more relaxed? Have your shoulders dropped a bit? The things you notice may seem small, but pay attention to them because they all add up. Write down in your notebook anything that you notice. And don't forget, you are the one who made these changes happen!

At first, some people try too hard when they do the Quick Coherence technique. They might wonder, *Am I doing it right? Am I thinking about appreciating my friend, or am I really feeling appreciation? Which source of appreciation should I choose—my dog, my friend, or my favorite grandmother? Do I still have mind chatter? What are the steps?* It takes a little practice to get the hang of it. The more you do it, though, the easier it becomes.

As you can see, the Quick Coherence technique is quite simple. But when the heat is on, it can be challenging to do it in the moment when you need it the most. Just like anything worthwhile you do, it takes practice. After all, you probably didn't ride your bike smoothly the first time you got on it. You likely had training wheels, and then when the training wheels came off, someone held on to the seat as you pedaled to help you balance. Once you practiced enough, you found your balance and off you went all by yourself. The same can happen with the Quick Coherence technique.

Take a few minutes to think about times when doing the Quick Coherence technique might be helpful. Write your ideas in your notebook. Here are some suggestions:

* before and during a test

* if you feel a little "off" but don't know why

* if you feel bored

* if you're having trouble focusing

* when studying

* when you first wake up in the morning

* when you just want to feel a good feeling for no particular reason at all

* when you see someone who irritates you

* when you take a shower

* when you're about to have what might be a tough or awkward conversation with someone

* while riding to school

* while you walk down the hall to your next class

Be sure to come up with a plan of how you will remind yourself to practice Quick Coherence. Some people find it helps to write reminders on sticky notes and put them on their bathroom mirror, refrigerator, locker door, or in their school notebook—somewhere you will see them often. Some people set alarms on their cell phones to go off as reminders. See what creative ways you can come up with that make sense to you.

Sometimes it may seem like not much is going on when you shift into a coherent state, but there really is a lot happening. It's a bit like your cell phone. Let's say you plug your cell phone in to recharge it. It doesn't seem like much is happening. After all, your phone just lies there on your desk, quietly charging. If you want to be able to use it later, you leave it plugged in so it will have a full charge. When you're in a coherent state, you are charging up your vitality and inner battery so you have more reserves, more energy to draw on when you need it later on.

Before going on, it's important that we acknowledge that many teens face some very difficult situations; maybe you're one of those teens. Because of that, you may find it more difficult to experience a renewing emotion. After all, when you're really angry, anxious, afraid, or sad, a renewing emotion might seem impossible to feel in that moment. You are just trying to survive! We understand that. In moments like these, do Heart-Focused Breathing. That can lower *some* of the emotional intensity and can help make the situation *more* manageable. We'll introduce another coherence-building technique in chapter 4 called Attitude Breathing, which some people find helpful when their emotions are intense.

Transforming Stress: Heart-Brain Coherence in Action

Now we'll take a look at how your brain and heart can promote coherence by working together. How well they work together has a whole lot to do with whether you feel a lot of stress or not. Let's see how heart-brain coherence worked for sixteen-year-old Danielle when she was faced with a tough situation at home.

> *When my parents first told me that they were going*
> *to split up, my heart wanted badly for them to be okay*
> *because I love them so much and I didn't want them to*
> *suffer. I started thinking about their separation and that*
> *triggered some different emotions. I was afraid of the*

future and kept remembering all the good times we had experienced in the past, which I thought would be lost forever. The more I thought, the more intense my emotions got. Soon I was totally lost in an ocean of overwhelming emotions and felt completely confused. I let my emotions of fear, disappointment, and loss get so blown up that I couldn't even talk about how deeply I cared about them and the love I had for them. Instead, when I would try to talk to them, I would get more frustrated and angry, and it would end up in a mess of misunderstanding. After wearing myself out from these strong emotions, I finally had nowhere else to go but to my heart.

I started seeing that the best way to talk to my parents would only be if I kept my emotions under control. When I did this, I had more clarity and could say what I really felt in my heart—that I was scared and sad and didn't know what to do. They could then better understand what I really felt and wanted to say to them. My relationship with them became more of what I wanted as I kept practicing this every time I talked with them. I was still sad, but together we could have a better conversation without blame and emotion getting in the way.

Emotions by themselves are not good or bad. They can add meaning to our lives and lighten the load we sometimes feel like we're carrying. But if we don't keep them balanced and under control, they can easily create confusion, lack of self-confidence, or uncertainty and give us a real energy-burning workout.

As we saw in Danielle's story, thoughts can trigger all sorts of emotions—such as anger, hurt, and anxiety—that don't feel good. But when you get your heart and brain working together as Danielle did, then your thoughts and emotions can work for you instead of against you.

Here's another example to help you understand how the brain and heart work together—or don't, as the case may be! This is seventeen-year-old Jonathan's story:

About a month ago, I was late getting to school every day for four days. My first period teacher was on my case and finally gave me a tardy notice. On Friday morning, I made sure I was ready so I could get there on time. I was on the way to school when we got caught in a traffic jam. The way the traffic was moving, I knew it was going to take a lot longer to get to school. I started thinking, I'll never make it on time! The one day I make an extra effort, and now this! I felt like giving everyone the finger and yelling and swearing. I felt frustrated and impatient, and I just knew my teacher wouldn't believe me.

All that emotion was rising inside me. I realized I was wasting a lot of energy on something—the traffic jam—that I couldn't change in that moment. I was also making an assumption about my teacher's reaction before I explained it to her. About the only thing I could change was to go to my heart and realize that I'm here and I just have to wait for the traffic to move. When I get to school, I'll explain what happened. Just remembering to go to my heart helped me feel calmer. In my heart, I knew that reacting wouldn't make the traffic move faster. So why feel uptight and start my day off with an edgy feeling? Besides, I remembered hearing that doctors and scientists have proven that when your emotions go into negative reactions, certain hormones are released that have a bad effect on your body. That reactive energy can build up over time and cause health problems. By taking a moment to remember to go to my heart, I saw the situation in a new way. My heart said, Hey, maybe this traffic jam could be used for a little time to slow down and get calm. The rest of the day will be really busy. Then I could handle the rest of my day, talking with my teacher, and whatever else might come up.

As you can see in Jonathan's story, he could respond in two different ways: (1) react, get angry, and yell at the driver whose flat tire or accident caused the traffic jam, or (2) calm down, get more balanced, and make peace with the situation. His story illustrates how you actually *do* have a choice in how you respond.

When you're upset about something, it's really not the issue or situation itself that's bothering you or causing the inner turmoil. It's the emotional importance or "significance" that you give the issue that determines the feeling of stress. You feel upset because your mind and emotions interpret the facts of the issue in a certain way and you assign it personal meaning. Here's an example:

At school, you go to your locker and two guys are talking nearby. You hear one guy talking about how upset he is because he didn't make the team and how unfair it is that someone else did. According to the guy speaking, the people who made the team are just not as talented as he is. You keep listening to how upset he is and all the reasons why he should have made the team instead of the others. It is obvious that he's really upset. As you listen, you probably don't feel those same feelings of being upset because you have not made the issue personal. You may even think, *I can understand why he's upset, but it seems he's making it a much bigger deal than it really is.* And yet, to him, it is a big deal because making the team means a lot to him. As we learned earlier, the heart and the brain are connected. So, all of this guy's depleting emotions were being communicated from his heart to his brain, resulting in incoherent heart rhythms—those herky-jerky, chaotic rhythms that we saw on that graph earlier in the chapter. Without knowing it, his depleting emotions were causing wear and tear on his body, including the dumping of stress hormones into it.

When you compare the first two stories above with this last one, you can see that it's the *meaning* you give to a situation that causes the inner turmoil and upset. The more you feed the issue with all the head thoughts and justifications, the bigger it gets—and that keeps you from being able to see the situation clearly. Sometimes the meaning you give to a situation is linked to something that happened earlier in your life—what we call *emotional memories.*

The Challenge of Emotional Memories

We've talked about the importance of taking charge of your emotions so that you not only can better handle stressful situations but so you can also feel better and enjoy life more. But even with your best efforts, does it ever feel like emotions "just happen" and you get hijacked by them?

Let's talk briefly again about your equipment upstairs—your brain. With a better understanding about how your brain works, you'll see that emotional memories can trigger a lightning-fast emotional reaction that can pack a powerful punch, seemingly out of nowhere. Have you ever had that happen? Many times these automatic reactions, however, are not an appropriate or best way to respond to the current situation. When you get triggered in this way—it happens to everyone at one time or another—it can be an unexpected jolt that leaves you feeling stressed out. More than likely, you don't handle the situation very well because your smart-thinking brain has gone offline.

Let's look closer at what happens. Emotional memories can be triggered by something that is happening now that is *similar* to something that happened in the past, even years ago. You might not even consciously remember what happened in the past. The feeling pops in so fast that your brain doesn't have time to understand what's different about the current situation and the situation in the past. Without thinking, you react. More than likely, you don't handle the current situation very well.

When you experience a strong emotion, a part of your brain remembers it, along with details connected with the event. For example, if a "big guy" bullied you in the past and you were angry and fearful in response to being bullied, you may feel those same feelings when you see other "big guys"—even if they are nice people with no intent to bully you. The smell of a hot dog might make you sick to your stomach because you came down with the stomach flu after eating one in the past. You may be afraid of dogs because when you were little a big dog barked and scared you, even if you don't remember it. In each case, an emotional memory was formed and "stored" in your brain. It's called the "fast-track brain circuit" because it happens faster than you can think about what's happening and you simply react.

There is another track called the "slow-track circuit" in your brain. Here the information about the "big guy" goes through a different brain pathway that lets you know that this guy is actually friendly and there is no reason to feel afraid. However, even if this happens, the feeling of fear that was triggered through the fast track has already sent signals causing your heart rhythms to become incoherent as well as stress hormones to be released into your body.

These two circuits operate continuously and simultaneously. Anytime you are triggered, Heart-Focused Breathing can quickly put the brakes on the fast-track, automatic response. If you do this often enough, you can stop the old, automatic fast-track responses like anger or anxiety, and gradually you may find that you can replace those old responses with calm or confidence, which then becomes your new automatic response. Of course, there are going to be some reactions that will take several attempts to stop the momentum of the automatic response, but getting back to balance *sooner* is a big step. Because the old response may have been around a long time, it will take practice, but don't underestimate even a little progress! Any progress you make is important and builds the foundation for more progress and for lasting change.

You've also learned the Quick Coherence technique, which can be effective to stop automatic responses. Most important is to choose a technique and use it! It takes practice at first, but each time you practice a technique, you build your self-control muscle, which will make practicing it more effective.

✳✳✳

So now you can see that depleting emotions not only feel lousy and drain your inner battery (and therefore your resilience), but they also create incoherence in your heart rhythms that in turn affects how clearly you think, communicate, and make decisions. All too often messes are created when we respond reactively. On the other hand, you can build your resilience by generating renewing emotions—which recharge your battery— with the Quick Coherence technique; by doing this, you can shift gears from depletion to inner renewal. You will feel better and be able to handle situations more effectively. All in all, it's important to recognize that you have a choice of how to respond to any situation and that the more resilience you build, the better you will be able to handle daily challenges, including making better decisions.

In the next chapter, we're going to introduce a tool called the Emotional Landscape. It can help you see how the wide range of emotions you experience affects your body. It's a valuable tool you'll be able to use every day.

Your Stress-Bustin', Resilience-Boostin', On-the-Go Action Plan

1. Pay attention every day to what you are feeling, especially feelings that drain your inner battery. Remember, it's not just the big emotional reactions that drain your battery. Pay attention to the smaller ones, such as feeling bored, with-drawn, sad, lonely, or even what feels like a minor frustra-tion. Those quiet drains can really add up. Noticing your emotions is an ongoing practice because it helps you become more aware of them. Once you are aware of them, you can use the techniques in this book to take charge of how you handle them.

2. Practice the Quick Coherence technique several times every day. Practice it when you don't feel any stress so that doing the technique becomes easier and more automatic. Especially practice using Quick Coherence as soon as you start to feel any depleting emotion.

    a. How will you remind yourself to practice the Quick Coherence technique throughout the day? Any kind of reminder is really helpful, including placing sticky notes where you will see them, setting an alarm on your phone, or creating a daily routine such as practicing in the car, right after lunch, every time you see a teacher who bothers you, or before a specific class.

    b. Pay attention to how you feel after you use the technique. Write this down in your notebook.

3. For the situation that you committed to "taking on" at the end of chapter 1, use the Quick Coherence technique. Practice shifting your depleting emotions to a renewing emotion when dealing with this situation.

chapter 3

The Emotional Landscape
Understanding How Emotions Affect Your Body

We all experience a wide array of emotions, including anger, calm, sadness, joy, irritation, boredom, appreciation, and many others. This range of emotions is what we refer to as our *emotional landscape*. The range of our emotions, and also how they change throughout the day, is part of what makes life so interesting and, at times, so challenging.

Emotions often seem strange and unpredictable. At times, they come out of nowhere at lightning-fast speed. Some—like anger—are loud and easy to see, while others—like boredom—are more subtle and can be more difficult to identify or pin down. Sometimes our emotions don't seem to make sense, and we wish they would just "go away." Sometimes they distract us when we are trying hard to focus on something else—like schoolwork.

Even though emotions can feel like a pain at times, they also can be really helpful. If you think about it, don't our emotions tell us whether we like or dislike something, are comfortable or uncomfortable, feel safe or unsafe? Without the experience of emotion, we would not be motivated to take action. Scientists even say that emotions play an important role in our survival. Without fear, for example, we would not try to avoid serious danger.

But, as you may be starting to see, some of our emotional responses are too reactive and immature. A few of them really need to be better managed if we are going to be our best more often! We may at times, for example, find ourselves stuck over and over again in the same emotional rut, and this rut does not serve us well. Maybe we are easily angered, constantly anxious, overly dramatic, frequently frustrated, or chronically depressed. While emotions are neither good nor bad, some of them do need our attention if we are going to be our best selves.

So, how do you deal with all these emotions, especially the ones that need a bit of managing? One way is to use a great visual tool called the Emotional Landscape. It's a diagram that helps you become aware of the wide range of emotions you experience each day and how these emotions can affect you. This chapter will teach you how to use the Emotional Landscape. Why is this important? Well, everyone experiences a big mixture of emotions in response to life's events. However, as we mentioned earlier, emotions can affect you far more than you realize. They can influence whether or not you have brain fog and muddled thinking. They determine if your nervous system is amped up or calmed down, or even if you are bathing your-self in stress hormones. Emotions can strongly affect how you respond to a situation—whether you blurt out something that gets you in trouble or respond in a more responsible, mature way. They can even influence how deeply you sleep and how fast you actually fall asleep.

So, given how important emotions are in life, understanding the Emotional Landscape diagram and learning how to use it can be very helpful. Here are some ways it can help you:

* to identify the many different emotions you experience each day, both the ones that drain your battery and the ones that renew you

* to see which emotions you experience most often

* to figure out if you spend more time draining your inner battery than you realize

* to understand how different emotions affect your body

* to set goals for stopping energy drains and recharging your battery

* to realize that even though you're relaxed and chilled, you still may be draining your battery

* to learn how using the techniques in this book can help you decrease stress both on the spot and overall as well as help you to be more resilient

Understanding the Emotional Landscape

The Emotional Landscape is a diagram that you can use to gain important information about and insight into how your emotions affect you. Take a look at the diagram below. We'll walk you through it so you'll understand it, and then we'll teach you how to use it.

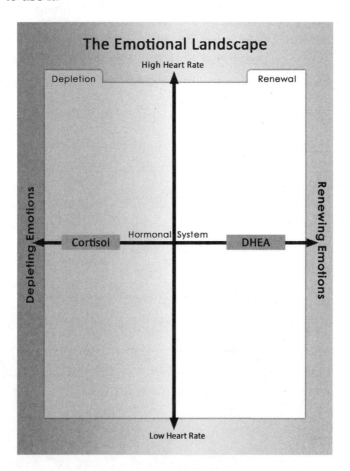

Range of Emotions: Depleting and Renewing

First, you'll see that the diagram is divided into four quadrants. Take a look at the two quadrants on the left side: near the top of the diagram, you'll see the label "Depletion" and along the left side, you'll see the label "Depleting Emotions." These are the emotions that you experience when you're stressed. They also can drain your inner battery if left unmanaged. They make you feel pretty lousy, too. The right two quadrants are labeled "Renewal" (near the top) and "Renewing Emotions" (along the right side) because they change what's happening in your body and actually have a renewing effect on you. The emotions that fall into the two right quadrants feel good and also charge up your inner battery.

Heart Rate

Now look for the arrow that goes from top to bottom: it indicates heart rate. You'll see that the upper two quadrants are labeled "High Heart Rate" and the lower two quadrants are labeled "Low Heart Rate." When your heart rate is high (upper quadrants), it's like you're stepping on the gas pedal in a car, which burns more gas. Only in this case, it's your own energy that you are burning. This is because your nervous system is revved up, which is indicated by your high heart rate. When your heart rate is lower (lower quadrants), however, it's like you're stepping on the brake, which means you aren't using as much energy. Your nervous system is not revved up. Your internal system slows down, just like a car slows down when the brake is applied.

Hormonal System

The Landscape also shows what type of hormones you're producing and that are circulating in your body. (See the horizontal arrow labeled "Hormonal System" across the middle of the diagram.) Hormones are chemicals that have many important functions in your body such as regulating your metabolism, organ functions, and body temperature. Hormones also affect your sleep and emotions. Some hormones have a long-lasting effect—that is, they affect your body for hours after they are produced. One of these is cortisol, which is known as the main stress hormone. You see it labeled on the left side of the diagram. When you experience depleting emotions (left two quadrants), your body produces more cortisol. As we just mentioned, cortisol can affect your body for hours after it is released. It is also well known that increased cortisol can keep you from sleeping well. When you find it difficult to sleep and you toss and turn a lot, you probably wake up feeling tired because you didn't get the full renewing effects of good sleep. As a result, your inner battery isn't getting recharged, and your resilience is low, making it more difficult to handle things that come up. You might feel more tension or irritation, and you may become overwhelmed more easily—in other words, stressful feelings start building up.

Now look at the right side of the diagram where you'll see the letters DHEA. That stands for dehydroepiandrosterone, so you can see why we just say "DHEA"! DHEA is also a hormone, but it has a very different effect on your body than cortisol has. DHEA has a renewing effect and is commonly known as the "vitality hormone." When you experience renewing emotions that fall on the right side of the Landscape, your body produces more DHEA.

We need both cortisol and DHEA for healthy functioning. We're better off, though, when they are in balance without too much of one or the other.

Your Emotional Landscape

Now that you have the lay of the Emotional Landscape, let's see how the emotions you experience each day fit into the four quadrants. We'll walk you through this step by step. You'll want to get out your notebook and draw a picture of the Landscape. Give yourself plenty of room. (Or, if you prefer, you can download a copy of the Emotional Landscape diagram from http://www.newharbinger.com/31946.)

As a quick review, the two upper quadrants are like stepping on the gas pedal and you burn more energy; this can rapidly drain your inner battery because you have a higher heart rate. The lower two quadrants mean you're not burning as much energy. The left two quadrants are for emotions that have a depleting effect on you and the right two quadrants are for emotions that feel good and renew you.

As you do the following exercise, remember that emotions are not good or bad, right or wrong. You're human and you're going to experience lots of different emotions. Everyone experiences lots of them—every day! Different emotions, however, affect you differently. That's what the Landscape will help you see. It's also a good way to inventory all the emotions you tend to experience during the day.

"When I see I'm on the left side of the Landscape, I know I don't have to stay there and I do Quick Coherence. It makes me feel calm and like I am more confident. I try to be on the right side as much as I can. I just have to remember to do a technique."

"Sometimes, I get stuck in the left quadrants for hours because I feel angry, annoyed, or at times lonely. Sooner or later, I realize that I am going nowhere and I use one of the techniques to get out of the rut."

Exercise: Mapping Your Emotional Landscape

Part 1: Identify Your Depleting Emotions

Step 1: Begin in the upper-left quadrant. This quadrant is for strong depleting emotions; they drain a lot of energy, sometimes very rapidly. The emotions people describe here are usually the ones they experience when they are "triggered"—emotions like anger, fear, impatience, irritation, frustration, anxiety, rage, and being overwhelmed.

What strong depleting emotions have you experienced in the last couple of days? Did you get *angry* about something or feel really *embarrassed* in a situation? Did you feel *overwhelmed* by your schoolwork or *anxious* because you felt like you didn't fit in? List your strong depleting emotions in the upper-left quadrant.

Step 2: The lower-left quadrant is for "quieter" depleting emotions, such as feeling worried, sad, bored, helpless, numb, lonely, or depressed. You probably can think of others.

What "quieter" depleting emotions have you experienced in the last couple of days? Did you feel *bored* in a class, or feel *lonely* because you're in a new school, or *sad* because you feel like you just don't fit in? List your quieter depleting emotions in the lower-left quadrant.

Part 2: Identify Your Renewing Emotions

Step 1: The lower-right quadrant is for "quieter" renewing emotions. These are emotions that feel good. Some examples are peace, contentment, appreciation, care, love, calm, and fulfillment.

What "quieter" renewing emotions have you experienced in the last couple of days? Did you feel *love* for your pet when he greeted you when you came home? Did you feel *appreciation* because someone helped you with a project? Did you feel *calm* or *peaceful* while taking a walk outdoors? List your quieter renewing emotions in the lower-right quadrant.

Step 2: And finally, the upper-right quadrant is for strong renewing emotions where you feel energized. These are emotions such as joy, happiness, enthusiasm, passion, or courage.

What strong renewing emotions have you experienced in the last couple of days? Did you feel *happy* when you hung out with friends? Did you feel *enthusiastic* when you got some good news about something important to you? List your strong renewing emotions in the upper-right quadrant. One thing to mention here is that if you stay feeling enthusiastic, excited, or joyful too long, it can also gradually drain you because your heart rate is higher. Your heart rate is a good indicator of how much energy your body is using.

Part 3: Reflect on Your Emotions

Step 1: After listing in the quadrants the emotions you've experienced recently, ask yourself, *What emotion(s) do I experience often?* Circle them.

Step 2: Then ask yourself, *In which quadrant(s) do I spend the most time?* Put an X in the applicable quadrant(s). There's no right or wrong answer. Be really honest with yourself so you can see where you might be draining (left quadrants) or recharging (right quadrants) your inner battery.

Step 3: Next, write the word "Goal" in the quadrant where you would like to spend more time. If you said you'd like to be on the right side of the Landscape more often—and who wouldn't?!—why would you like to be there? Is it because it simply feels better to go through your day feeling renewing emotions like happiness, contentment, peace, calm, enthusiasm, or appreciation? That's a great reason. But what are some other reasons? Write your reasons in your notebook.

Great! You now have mapped out the emotions you've experienced recently. But let's not stop there. There is one more important step! Because it's so important, we're going to spend a little time explaining it first. After all, if you found you experienced emotions that put you on the depleting side of the Landscape (and everyone has), let's see how to shift to the renewing side. That's you taking charge of you on the spot. That's maturity.

Using the Techniques to Shift on the Landscape

Recall that we said practicing Heart-Focused Breathing helps turn down the emotional intensity when you get triggered. For example, let's say someone says something to you that really gets under your skin and makes you feel angry. You're fuming! Feeling angry puts you in the upper-left quadrant of the Emotional Landscape diagram. You experience a rapid energy burn because anger is such a depleting emotion that can get your heart and brain out of sync, which makes it more difficult to think clearly and respond appropriately to a situation. Later, after you've calmed down, you may even feel tired—an indication of how the anger drained your battery.

The good news is that by practicing Heart-Focused Breathing (chapter 1) you can turn down the intensity of your reaction and shift to the lower-left quadrant, which means you're saving a lot of energy! It also means you've put the brakes on how you respond to the situation. You may still feel some anger—only it's not as intense; it's a "quieter" anger. But even quieter anger is depleting, so how do you get from the left quadrant to the right—from a depleting to a renewing emotion?

Remember that to be on the right side of the Landscape means you have to *feel* or *experience* a renewing emotion. To do that, you can use the Quick Coherence technique (chapter 2) to genuinely experience a renewing emotion. You can learn to get coherent and spend more time on the right side of the Landscape. It's *you* taking charge of how you respond and how you feel in any moment.

Heart Rhythms and Your Emotional Landscape

Do you remember our discussion in chapter 2 of coherent and incoherent heart rhythms? When you do the Quick Coherence technique, your heart rhythm pattern changes from an incoherent pattern to a coherent one—from chaotic to smooth and rolling. You shift from the left to the right side of the Landscape.

If you were hooked up to a heart rhythm monitor, you would be able to see that your heart rhythms become more coherent as you experience a renewing emotion.

Creating a coherent heart rhythm sends signals to your brain that help bring your smart-thinking brain back online so you can think more clearly even while taking a test, doing homework, or deciding the best way to handle a communication issue with a friend or family member. When your smart-thinking brain is online, you are more focused and can make better decisions. If you think about it, this should be an important skill to develop considering the fact that you make hundreds of decisions every day.

Being able to think clearly, make good decisions, and communicate well is everyday stuff. Clearly, as you spend more time on the right side of the Landscape, you probably will get along better with other people. You also will have a greater ability to be in charge of how you handle situations. It's better to be in charge of *how* you respond in a situation than reacting by throwing a fit, saying things you'll later regret, or making a decision that gets you in trouble.

Here is a key point to remember: *Feeling* renewing emotions is what puts you on the renewing (right) side of the Landscape. It's not so much thinking good thoughts or visualizing something pleasant as it is *feeling* renewing emotions, which creates a coherent heart rhythm pattern and a more optimal internal state so you can be at your best more often. To help you remember this, pull out the Emotional Landscape diagram that you created in the exercise above. Next we'll give you a couple more things we want you to do with the Landscape.

Exercise: Mapping Your Emotional Landscape—Continued

Part 4: Heart Rhythms

Step 1: Across the middle of the left side of the Landscape from right to left (along the line that separates the upper-left quadrant from the lower-left quadrant), draw a herky-jerky line. (It should look something like the incoherent heart rhythm pattern in the graph in chapter 2.) When you're hanging out in the left two quadrants, your heart rhythms are incoherent and look chaotic, just like the line you drew.

Step 2: Across the middle of the right side of the Landscape from left to right (along the line that separates the upper-right quadrant from the lower-right quadrant), draw a line that looks like smooth rolling hills and valleys. (It should look like the coherent heart rhythm pattern in the graph in chapter 2.) Your heart rhythm pattern becomes smooth and ordered, coherent, when you're on the right side.

Now that you are getting the hang of how to use the Landscape, use it often! You might even draw the diagram in the corner of a test you're taking. It just might remind you—if you start feeling anxious (left side)—to practice Quick Coherence so you can get your smart-thinking brain back online. That's how practical it can be to use. Using the diagram is also a good way to see if you may be on the depleting side more than you realize, as many people discover.

Now that you have a good feel for how to use the Landscape, let's use it to illustrate one more very important point.

The Difference Between Relaxation and Coherence

It's not unusual to hear someone say, "Just chill out" when something unsettling happens. Being able to calm down and chill out is important, but it doesn't necessarily mean you feel much better. Let's use the Landscape to show you why.

When you're in the two lower quadrants of the Landscape, you're probably fairly relaxed and your heart beats more slowly. Notice, however, that if you are feeling sad, bored, or lonely (the lower-left quadrant), for example, you are still on the depleting side of the Landscape. As we have said before, those depleting emotions can negatively affect you if they are not managed. However, chilling out in the lower-left quadrant can mean that you just aren't burning as much energy, which is a good thing and a step in the right direction. Ideally, though, you can take another step to be on the right side—the renewing side—of the Landscape.

Being in the lower-left quadrant where you feel quiet depleting emotions is very different from the lower-right quadrant where you feel calm, peaceful, balanced, or content. For one thing, those renewing emotions feel much better than the emotions in the lower-left quadrant. Renewing emotions such as calm or peacefulness create a coherent heart rhythm pattern that helps bring your heart and brain in sync and brings your smart-thinking brain back online. It simply feels better to experience renewing emotions. In the lower-right quadrant, rather than producing stress hormones, you're producing those that have a renewing and regenerative effect on you.

Now that we've looked more closely at how the different emotions you experience every day affect you by using the Emotional Landscape, we're going to look more closely in the next chapter at something that often goes unnoticed, but which can have a big impact on whether or not you're feeling stress—your attitudes!

Stress-Bustin', Resilience-Boostin', On-the-Go Action Plan

1. Watch for those situations and events that trigger emotions that drain your inner battery, and be aware of where you are on the Emotional Landscape. Do this on the go throughout the day. Remember, it's not just the big emotional reactions that drain your battery and get your heart and brain out of sync. Don't forget the little ones, such as feeling lonely, bored, withdrawn, helpless, or a little bit frustrated. The small emotional reactions can be like a tiny pebble in your shoe. You might not really notice it at first, but the more you walk, the more the pebble rubs uncomfortably on a spot on your foot. Before you know it, you have a good-size blister. So catch the energy drains early by noticing them and then do Heart-Focused Breathing (chapter 1) or Quick Coherence (chapter 2)!

2. Also identify situations and events where you find yourself feeling renewed and on the right side of the Emotional Landscape. What emotions are you experiencing—peace, appreciation, gratitude, enthusiasm, calm, happiness? Practice

experiencing any of the renewing emotions you identify as you do the Quick Coherence technique.

3. By practicing the Heart-Focused Breathing and the Quick Coherence techniques, you take charge of how you respond and feel in any moment, so practice often! Don't wait for the big emotional blowouts to use a technique. Continue practicing the techniques several times every day. Practice when you aren't feeling stressed so using them becomes more automatic. Also practice one of the techniques as soon as you start to feel any stress-producing emotion.

   a. How will you remind yourself to practice a technique throughout the day?

   b. Pay attention to how you feel after you use the technique. You might want to write this down in your notebook.

4. For the situation that you committed to "taking on" at the end of chapter 1, try using the Quick Coherence technique and practice shifting your emotions to a renewing emotion when dealing with this situation. Use the Emotional Landscape to identify the emotions you experience before and after practicing Quick Coherence.

chapter 4

Positive Change
The Stress-Busting Power of a Shift in Attitude

Attitudes are the way people tend to think or feel about someone or something. You might think of attitudes as self-talk—conversations you have with yourself. Some attitudes are uplifting and make you feel good, such as when you tell yourself, *I can do it,* while other attitudes leave you feeling in a funk, such as when you mumble to yourself, *Poor me, I can't do anything right.* Attitudes and feelings go hand-in-hand.

Attitudes can become everyday habits, almost as automatic as picking up and holding your fork in your hand when you eat. You might not even notice the inner mumblings at first, probably because you've gotten so used to them. Or maybe you notice them all the time and they drive you crazy because you can't turn them off! And, just maybe, no one ever helped you take a close look at them so you could see how they color the way you see the world and how they can affect your relationships.

If you were to stop and truly pay attention, you might notice that attitudes can play repeatedly in your mind. You might mutter aloud, "He's no good and shouldn't have made the team" without even realizing you're doing it. Have you ever done that? You might stew about something someone said that made you feel hurt or disappointed and rehash it over and over, which makes you feel even worse. It can be difficult if not impossible to turn off this self-talk. In a similar way, you've probably observed your friends, classmates, parents, and teachers grumbling about the same thing again and again. We don't have to tell you that negative attitudes can create a lot of stress!

Sometimes it's clear when a person needs to change an attitude. Maybe you've heard someone say, "Girl, you need an attitude adjustment." Or you might say to a classmate, "You're always complaining about your math teacher and how unfair you think she is. You've got a real attitude problem." An attitude like that isn't going to help the situation, and a change of attitude is needed. By the way, teens aren't the only ones with griping and grumbling attitudes. Adults have them, too!

An interesting thing about attitudes and feelings—and something to be on the lookout for—is that it's very easy for your brain to justify them. Your brain will likely have no problem at all coming up with a list of reasons why you're justified to stew in self-pity or gripe about school.

For example, let's say a classmate did something that made you really mad. You sat there grumbling to yourself that what she did wasn't fair, it wasn't right, that she's stupid to behave that way, and that you wouldn't treat someone that way. For all of those reasons, you have the "right" to grumble and stew about her actions.

But here's the tricky thing: what good does that attitude do except keep the story alive, leaving you feeling miserable? If you recall from chapter 3, when you feel miserable, you're also producing stress hormones and your nervous system is revving up.

Not to mention that while you're stewing, the other person is probably out having a fun time and completely unaware of how you're feeling. Your poor-me attitude ends up hurting *you*. It also does nothing to help you find a way to work out the situation.

There are other negative attitudes besides the poor-me attitude. Here are some common ones:

* doubtfulness

* jealousy

* judgmentalism

* mean-spiritedness

* self-centeredness

* self-pity

* self-righteousness

* whining

You may have one of those attitudes as you think about a situation, another person, or even yourself. Attitudes can also be stories that you tell yourself about yourself. Here are a few examples:

* "I only care about myself."

* "Things always go wrong."

* "I can't do anything right."

* "Everything sucks!"

* "I hate him."

* "I'm smarter and better than everyone."

* "Everyone and everything is stupid."

* "I'm not as pretty/good looking as others."

* "I'm not smart enough to pass algebra."

* "No one likes me."

* "Compared to others, I'm a loser."

Or maybe you complain about things at school or at home:

* "I have way too much homework all the time. No one ever gives me a break."

* "I can't stand one of my teachers. She tries to act cool, but she's a loser."

* "That test was so unfair."

* "Everyone's on my case about everything."

* "It's not fair he made the team and I didn't."

* "My parents just don't understand me."

* "Everyone has a new smartphone except me."

> The greatest day in your life and mine is when we take total responsibility for our attitudes. That's the day we truly grow up.
> —John C. Maxwell

Although it might sound like a cliché, it *is* our attitude toward life's circumstances and challenges that can determine our future. Many studies show that our attitudes determine our degree of success in life. You may have noticed that people who have more inner strength and positive attitudes and feelings enjoy life more. They tend to be more successful than people who are down on life and complain about anything and everything. Attitudes can motivate us and provide energy, *real* energy, to accomplish the things that are important to us. Other attitudes, however, such as those listed above, can drag us down and take away not only our success, but also take away our personal fulfillment.

Exercise: Your Attitude Inventory

Think of this exercise as taking an inventory of your attitudes, especially the ones that play out as grumbles and gripes. Have fun with it. You might even find yourself laughing at some of your attitudes and the griping and grumbling you do! Be genuine, though, as you do the exercise. You may discover some attitudes you didn't realize you had.

- Take a few minutes in a quiet place and recall times when you've had a negative attitude about something, someone, or even yourself. See how many you can think of and write them down in your notebook. Refer to the lists of common negative attitudes above to give you some ideas.

- How do the attitudes you identified affect your relationships with your parents, friends, or teachers or how you feel about yourself?

- How often do these attitudes show up in your daily life? Do they last a couple minutes? All day? Do you find yourself griping about something that happened three weeks ago—or even longer?

The first step toward changing an attitude is to identify what needs to be changed, as you've done in the last exercise. When it comes to changing your attitude, an honest self-evaluation is a must. But in your self-evaluation, be sure to have some compassion for yourself. Why? Because you're not alone. Almost every human being has attitudes that get in the way of living life fully. Attitudes are simply learned behaviors that accumulate over time, and as you might be discovering, all too often they become automatic ways you think about something. In other words, grumbling seems to just happen! You may feel like you're stuck in a muddy rut, spinning your tires and going nowhere—except deeper into the hole of even more negativity. You don't have to keep spinning your wheels though, as you'll see shortly.

When you're first trying to name your negative attitudes, you may feel threatened or awkward about identifying an attitude that doesn't serve you well—an attitude such as telling yourself, *Everything I do is wrong*. It is part of growing and maturing where an old "skin"—your old attitude—is shed in favor of a newer one. For some, it might take real courage to shed an old skin, but the results will be worth it. Changing an attitude can feel like an uphill struggle or a do-good attempt at positive thinking with no juice behind it. You need power to change the momentum and make attitude shifts that are meaningful. So what can you do?

One thing you can do is practice Quick Coherence (chapter 2), which can help you quickly shift a feeling or an attitude. But there are times when you'll need extra power to shift from a deep-rutted draining attitude to a more positive attitude and to make it stick so you're genuinely free of that old attitude. You can add that power with a HeartMath technique called Attitude Breathing. With Attitude Breathing, you can change a negative attitude more quickly and find your way to a more positive attitude that can improve your outlook on a situation or about life in general.

Attitude Breathing Technique

The Attitude Breathing technique helps you stop negative attitudes and replace them with ones that boost your energy, clear your head, and freshen your outlook on life. Making this attitude shift will also lessen the amount of the stress hormone cortisol circulating in your body.

When you decide to use Attitude Breathing, you choose to make a positive difference for yourself. It's like changing your old inner story and writing a new story in that moment. This time it's a story that is stress-bustin' and resilience-boostin'! Attitude Breathing can help you get out of the "poor me" rut or any other negative attitude you might have. Moment by moment, you decide what new attitude or feeling you would like to have. And perhaps best of all, when you practice Attitude Breathing regularly, you gradually build the power to make attitude shifts that last.

Attitude Breathing requires that you choose an attitude— such as courage, patience, "I can," or "it's going to be a good week"—to draw into yourself. Don't worry if you can't find a new attitude or feeling right away or if you feel an inner resistance. Take your time and don't try to force anything to happen.

Now it's time to give Attitude Breathing a try. We'll give the technique first and then offer some tips for using it. Read through all of the steps at least once before you try the technique. Have your notebook ready. Be sure to write the replacement attitude you select in step 2 in your notebook as well as make notes of what you experience when you try the technique. (If you have difficulty coming up with a new attitude to replace a negative one, see the section below entitled "Replacing Negative Attitudes with Positive Attitudes.")

Technique: Attitude Breathing

Step 1: *Recognize a feeling or attitude that you want to change and identify a replacement attitude.*

Step 2: *Focus your attention in the area of the heart. Imagine your breath is flowing in and out of your heart or chest area, breathing a little slower and deeper than usual.*

Step 3: *Breathe the feeling of the new attitude slowly and casually through the heart area.*

Option: *Breathe two attitudes if you'd like. For example, breathe in an attitude of calm and breathe out an attitude of confidence, or breathe in an attitude of love and breathe out an attitude of compassion.*

Here are a few helpful tips to get the most out of Attitude Breathing:

- Inhale five seconds, exhale five seconds (or whatever rhythm is comfortable).

- Even if you can't feel the attitude shift at first, making a genuine effort to shift will help you to at least get to a neutral state. *Neutral* means that you've stopped the momentum of the negative attitude or feeling you want to change, even if you haven't yet genuinely shifted to a positive attitude. This can give you more objectivity and save your energy.

- Remember that justifying a negative attitude only keeps it alive. Have a genuine "I mean business" attitude to shift to a new, positive attitude. It could take a few minutes, but it's worth it.

- Notice even the smallest changes in your attitude. You might not be able to completely feel the new attitude at first, but making a genuine effort to bring about the inner shift can help you get to a neutral state, which can slow down or stop the old attitude in its tracks. That alone can be a big help! You'll save energy, too.

- When you first try Attitude Breathing, you might feel like you're going against what you know or think you know about a situation. Some attitudes and feelings are stubborn, and you've probably had them longer than you realize. That's when it can help to "put your heart into it" and have an "I can do" attitude. Just keep breathing the new attitude. Remember to breathe slowly and comfortably and stay focused on the new attitude or feeling even when you feel resistance. There's no need to force it to happen. Imagine pulling in and holding on to the new feeling in your heart.

- During strong emotional reactions, such as when someone says something that makes you angry, you may need to breathe the new attitude for two or three minutes before your nerves quiet down and you experience a shift. That's okay! Take the time you need in order to feel the new attitude "take hold." You might want to do it several times.

Now give Attitude Breathing a try for two to three minutes. If possible, you might want to practice this in a quiet place where you won't be disturbed. (You also may want to review the steps one more time.) When you finish, reflect on your experience. What did you notice as you practiced it? Make notes of your experience in your notebook. Attitude Breathing is a simple but effective technique, so practice it a lot.

Replacing Negative Attitudes with Positive Attitudes

To help jump-start the process to the practice of Attitude Breathing, take a look at the following two lists to give you some ideas of common negative attitudes and some suggested positive feelings and attitudes to replace them—right there on the spot! You can think of replacement attitudes as being opposites of the unwanted ones. These are only suggestions. You might have a sense of one that works better. Go with it!

Negative Attitudes and Feelings	Positive Replacement Attitudes and Feelings
Angry/Upset	Breathe calm or neutral to cool down
Anxious	Breathe calm
Bored	Breathe responsibility or creativity
Fatigued	Breathe increased energy or vitality
Fearful	Breathe courage, peace, or calm
Fogged/Confused	Breathe clarity
"I can't"	Breathe "I can"
Impatient	Breathe patience

Isolated/Lonely	Breathe being connected, sociable, or appreciated
Judgmental	Breathe ease, tolerance, or compassion
Overwhelmed	Breathe ease or peace
Rebellious	Breathe respect or calm
Self-pity/Poor me	Breathe maturity, confidence, or strength
Shamed/Guilty	Breathe kindness, care, or compassion to yourself
Stressed	Breathe calm or ease
Uncertain	Breathe patience

Can you think of other negative attitudes that you experience? If you can't think of any others right now, be on the lookout for them. See which positive replacement attitudes give you the most relief and write them down. As you practice, you'll discover that each positive replacement attitude has a different feeling that helps you get the stress out.

Attitude Breathing and the Emotional Landscape

Take a look again at the list of Negative Attitudes and Feelings and Positive Replacement Attitudes and Feelings above. Let's see how the attitudes in each column fit into the Emotional

Landscape diagram that we discussed in chapter 3. As you read down the list of Negative Attitudes and Feelings, what effect do they have on your inner battery? They drain your energy, right? You could put that entire list on the left side—the depleting side—of the Landscape. As you can probably guess, each of the negative attitudes and feelings creates an incoherent heart rhythm. Remember that an incoherent heart rhythm sends signals to the brain and takes your smart-thinking brain offline. When that happens, it's difficult to work through a situation, and, in fact, you likely will end up with even more unwanted, negative attitudes that further drain your inner battery. You just can't be your best on the left side of the Landscape!

So what about the positive replacement attitudes and feelings? They all go on the right side of the Landscape, right? For one, they feel a lot better. They also create a coherent heart rhythm, which sends ordered signals to your brain, bringing it back online. Rather than draining your inner battery, you're recharging it. You can be at your best more often.

Attitude Breathing, then, is another technique that can help you shift from the left side to the right side of the Landscape. Attitude Breathing helps put you in charge of how you respond so that you—not those automatic attitudes—run the show.

"It takes practice, but Attitude Breathing really helps me stay more calm and less anxious when talking to different people at school."

"For as long as I can remember, I get mad and frustrated when things don't go my way. It gets me in trouble. Now I use Attitude Breathing to try and calm myself down. I breathe in calm. Most of the time, it helps a lot."

Attitude Breathing in Daily Life

It can be fun to experiment with different attitudes, especially when you are stealthily practicing the Attitude Breathing technique around people at school or at home. With practice, you will develop new awareness of what each attitude feels like and what it can do for you. Practice Attitude Breathing until you remember to do it automatically when you feel irritated, frustrated, angry, anxious, or fearful. Here are some ideas of when you might practice Attitude Breathing during the day:

* Breathe courage if you feel fear.

* Breathe clarity if you feel confused about your homework.

* Breathe calm or clarity before and while taking a test.

* Breathe confidence before a difficult situation or conversation.

* Breathe patience when someone annoys you.

* Breathe peace when you feel the hurt from an old situation that you can't change.

* Breathe strength when you feel fear or apprehension about a situation to center yourself and prepare for whatever might happen next. It might not be as bad as you think it will be.

Do Attitude Breathing several times during the day—even when nothing is disturbing you—in order to build up a storage bank of energy. The advantage of stored energy is that it helps lift you above frustrations, anxieties, and gridlocks in day-to-day life that would otherwise drain you. It gives you a chance to sort out challenges without them taking you down. When these stressors take you off guard, and they will from time to time, take a moment and use Attitude Breathing.

The great thing about Attitude Breathing is that you can literally do it on the go. During the day if you notice any negative attitudes, thoughts, or emotions, take a moment to focus on a positive replacement attitude and then practice Attitude Breathing again. Learn to practice Attitude Breathing while you're walking down the hall, doing your homework, or hanging out with friends. As with any of the techniques in this book, you don't have to stop what you're doing to use Attitude Breathing. And keep in mind that a lot of your energy drains away when you get sucked into other people's drama. Sincere practice of Attitude Breathing can help change this or at least cushion you from getting whacked by someone else's lousy attitude. Positive thinking alone is not enough to shift attitudes that are highly charged with emotion. Adding heart coherence is the missing factor, because it puts energy behind the intent.

And after you've been on the go all day, Attitude Breathing can help you end your day on an uplifting note. Focusing on a positive replacement attitude when you go to bed can lead to more peaceful and deeper sleep, reducing the carryover of emotional turmoil accumulated from the day. Breathe balance, ease, appreciation, or any replacement attitude for a few minutes after you close your eyes or until you fall asleep.

Just as you can use Attitude Breathing on the go throughout the day, you can also use it to prepare in advance for situations, encounters, and events that you may be concerned about. Let's look first at general prepping and then prepping for your day.

Prepping with Attitude Breathing

Let's say tomorrow you have a test and you get anxious or nervous on test days. Practicing Attitude Breathing today can help you get calm now, which can make it easier both to get calm when you sit down to take the test and to remain calmer during the test. Of course, positive attitudes are not just for getting ready for taking tests. They can help prepare you for any encounters with people, issues, or situations that trigger stress for you. Practicing Attitude Breathing builds your resilience, which means you can be better prepared for unexpected situations that might be stressful. Try breathing attitudes of calm, compassion, courage, forgiveness, or patience that give you emotional strength. By breathing these attitudes, you store energy so you have it when you need it.

Prepping for Your Day

You can also use Attitude Breathing to prep for your day. Start the day with Attitude Breathing as soon as you get out of bed. Negative thoughts, attitudes, and emotions like worry, sadness, hurt, or anger often creep in as soon as you wake up in the morning and sometimes before you even get out of bed. That's where the expression "getting up on the wrong side of the bed" comes from. That's not a great way to start the day.

Breathe appreciation or calm while you're getting dressed, making breakfast, or getting ready for school. When you get distracted, just remember to go back and practice Attitude

Breathing instead of rehashing situations in your mind. With sincere practice, this technique can prevent your emotions from becoming frayed, helping you rise above the grind of daily living. You can use Attitude Breathing before any situation that might be stressful.

Remember, it's not the situation itself that drains you. It's the repetitive thoughts and emotional oversignificance you give to those situations that depletes your energy. Typically, it's the little stuff that gets blown out of proportion that then becomes big stuff. Practice taking the significance out of negative thoughts, feelings, and attitudes. You can do that by breathing in the attitude of "taking significance out" or "no big deal," which then can cut short your journey down the stress highway. Having a "no big deal" attitude can also help in other challenging situations that we'll talk about next.

Using Attitude Breathing with Painful Experiences

It's understandable that you would feel upset from a past situation that caused you hurt or pain. But that doesn't mean you can't begin to release the hold that hurt and pain have on you. Your heart can open you to new insights that will help release those feelings and help you see the situation with clarity and balance. When situations come up that trigger negative attitudes, breathe in a replacement attitude to clear out the negativity, which will help ease the grip that the old attitude has on you.

When memories of more traumatic situations or events resurface, use Attitude Breathing for a few moments to stop the momentum of the memories from building. Regular practice of any of the techniques—Heart-Focused Breathing (chapter 1), Quick Coherence (chapter 2), or Attitude Breathing—can lessen the impact of traumatic memories and, over time, help you build healthier responses.

Transforming Negative Attitudes

It's important to understand that Attitude Breathing doesn't sweep negative attitudes under the rug. Instead, it helps transform them. You might think of this transformation as a process of befriending the negative attitude by bringing it into your heart—not fighting it—and holding it in your heart while releasing the significance you've attached to it. For example, let's say you've had the attitude for a long time that you just can't do anything right. To "befriend" the attitude is to acknowledge to yourself in all honesty, that's how you feel. That can help because you're not putting energy into holding it in. Sometimes that alone can take out some of its charge. Then breathe in a replacement attitude of how you really want to feel.

Sometimes, however, when you might prefer to hold on to a reaction or pout, or when a negative attitude "owns" you, go against the grain of habit and have a talk with yourself. Say to yourself that you're going to do something different for yourself and breathe in a positive attitude. You might decide one day—it might just be today—that you've simply had enough of draining emotional reactivity. That's a great attitude to have—enough already! That can give you a boost of energy and commitment to "take on" daily challenges.

You might also find that you're not the only one with attitudes that need changing. It can be helpful to realize that many and probably most people have their own day-to-day issues and challenges to handle. They, too, feel frustration, uncertainty, fear, anger, or rage. This can make everyone around you edgy and irritable. Have an attitude of compassion for yourself and others. You won't always know what someone else may be struggling with. As soon as you catch yourself getting irritated, frustrated, angry or full of rage, use Attitude Breathing to take out as much of the negative reaction as you can and shift into heart rhythm coherence. Anchoring or "settling in" your energy in your heart will help you stay centered so you can see these situations calmly and find a better way to respond.

Again, you aren't the only one with attitudes that don't serve you well. More than likely, almost everyone around has them, too. Now that you've read this chapter and better understand negative attitudes, start noticing if other people are grumbling. Pay attention to what it's like to be around people when they're griping about something someone said to them or about how unfair it was for the teacher to talk to them in a critical tone in front of everyone. How does another person's grumbling affect you? Is it annoying, irritating, and just not fun to be around? Of course! Who wants to be around that?

What commonly happens is that people can get pulled into someone else's grumbling, which then pulls you into the rut with them, and you end up spinning your tires together, going nowhere. Put on the brakes by practicing Attitude Breathing (or Heart-Focused Breathing, from chapter 1, or Quick Coherence, from chapter 2)—and maybe teach your friend how to do it, too. You'll both end up feeling better. You may end up laughing about all the grumbling you just did! Doing so can help keep other people's grumbling from getting under your skin.

Building Inner Security with Positive Attitudes

As you breathe in positive replacement attitudes with greater frequency, your inner security increases and you know better how to handle stressful situations. *Inner security* means being comfortable and confident with yourself so that you can respond appropriately rather than react to a situation. It is worth the effort it takes to build that sense of security. Without inner security, you can't be who you really are. In short, this entire book is about building inner security.

You can start increasing inner security by generating attitudes and feelings of courage, compassion, care, appreciation, forgiveness, and "I can"; these attitudes and feelings also increase heart coherence. They release different hormones, which feel better to your system. That's your body's way of saying, "Yes, I want to feel more of these attitudes." As you feel more secure, you see that you have a choice about the kinds of attitudes you experience: those that are more reactive and self-defeating such as anxiety, fear, irritation, or anger, or those that help you respond with greater poise, maturity, security, and awareness.

And don't forget to practice Attitude Breathing even when you're already feeling great. Doing so will add energy to your system, making it easier to bounce back when you do get knocked off your feet. If you keep practicing it, you may find you start doing it automatically. That's certainly a worthwhile goal!

You can see that attitudes, whether or not you are even aware of them, can be the source of a lot of stress. In the next chapter, we're going to talk about a fascinating topic, intuition, and how you can put your intuition to work for you to help you de-stress.

Your Stress-Bustin', Resilience-Boostin', On-the-Go Action Plan

1. Notice throughout the day feelings and attitudes that feel lousy. The lists of negative attitudes earlier in the chapter may give you some ideas, but there may be others you notice that are not on the lists. Then identify a replacement feeling or attitude.

2. Practice Attitude Breathing several times each day. Do it on the go. What do you notice when you do Attitude Breathing? Write down in your notebook some of the unwanted attitudes you experienced and also the replacement attitudes. Write down how the replacement attitudes were helpful.

3. Identify one situation or event that triggers unwanted attitudes frequently and commit to practicing Attitude Breathing for those attitudes. Breathing in a new attitude is like breathing in a new way to respond to the situation or event. Take your time as you practice Attitude Breathing.

chapter 5

Intuition
Listening to Your Heart

Have you ever known something about a person or situation without knowing how you knew it? Perhaps you had a gnawing feeling inside that you were forgetting something, and later on at school, you realized you left your homework on your bed. Have you ever had a weird feeling about a classmate, and later that day, you found out he was in some kind of trouble? Have you been in a situation where you started to say something and then you abruptly pulled back and did not say anything? Somehow, you knew the timing was not right. Or if you play sports, you suddenly knew just the right move to get yourself in position to score a goal.

In each case, a sense of knowing seemed to "come to you" out of nowhere. This sense of knowing is called *intuition*. New research shows that your heart plays a very important role in intuition. Later in this chapter, you will find out how intuition can be an important tool for dealing with stress. You will learn to develop your own intuition to help you make wiser choices about how you handle situations, which can lessen your stress.

But first, let's take a closer look at intuition, your heart, and what we mean by the "intelligence of the heart."

Intuition: The Intelligence of the Heart

Intuition doesn't have to be a mystery. Things are only a mystery until they're understood. When someone is trying to make a decision or figure out the best way to handle a situation, you've probably heard people say, "Follow your heart," "Listen to what your heart tells you," or "Your heart knows best." People instinctively know that their own heart is a source of wisdom and guidance; this is what we refer to as the *intelligence of the heart* or, simply, heart intelligence.

Too often people refer to the heart only when talking about babies, puppy dogs, greeting cards, and flowers. It's time to focus on the *intelligence* of the heart rather than on sentimental feelings and metaphors. Why? Because the heart offers a way to access your intuition, which in turn helps you to find the best way to handle a situation. Not only does the intelligence of your heart guide you along the way, but it also gives you the power and courage to follow through with choices you want to make. Heart intelligence allows you to more clearly see multiple points of view, giving you more options for handling situations and enabling you to make better choices.

"Don't let the noise of others' opinions drown out your own inner voice. And most important, have the courage to follow your heart and intuition. They somehow already know what you truly want to become. Everything else is secondary."—Steve Jobs, cofounder of Apple Inc.

Heart intelligence isn't only for times when you're down and out. When you live from your heart more often, you connect with your intuitive guidance more consistently. That helps you surf more smoothly through situations and challenges that come up throughout the day. It also powers up your creativity, giving you an extra boost to discover more of who you really are. When you follow your heart's intelligence throughout the day, you can *be* more of the person you truly are rather than feeling weighted down by all the stress you carry.

You may be wondering why so many people don't use their intuition more often if it's so natural. People tend to look at their intuition from the perspective of their thinking brain, the head, and not from their heart. That's why it's still a bit of a mystery to many people. When people talk about having a "flash of intuition" or a "flash of insight," they think it's coming from their head—and sometimes it is. But it's your heart that helps you *access* your intuition.

Three Types of Intuition

Research conducted on intuition at the HeartMath Institute Research Center, along with research by other scientists around the world, indicates that there are three basic types of intuition. More than likely you've experienced each of these without even knowing you have. You might think of intuition as an inner knowing—knowing something without knowing how you know it.

Because intuition is natural, people aren't really aware of what it is or how it works, and therefore, they tend to take it for granted. Let's begin by describing each type of intuition.

Implicit Knowledge

One type of intuition, *implicit knowledge,* works by your brain subconsciously comparing what is happening right now with stored memories of things you learned in the past. The term "implicit" refers to the kind of memories that we don't normally think about. This is similar to things you have learned that are now so familiar that you do them without thinking about it, like walking or riding a bike. Our brains have two different systems for analyzing all the information coming into them and figuring things out. One system is where we have to consciously stop and think about things, such as making a decision or solving a math problem, or when we have to carefully weigh things out. Another way the brain works is that it very quickly and automatically finds matches between previous experiences with what is going on right now, but without having to consciously stop and think about things. You just know what to do. For example, something inside you tells you to avoid someone because in the past you experienced him as having a lot of negativity. In this example, your previous experience laid down a memory track that sprang into action the moment you saw this person. That creates a choice point, which means you can consciously choose to react automatically to the old memory track, or choose to respond with a more appropriate and mature response.

Another aspect of implicit knowledge is where your brain works things out over hours or days. You've probably had this happen when all of sudden, for example, you remembered the right answer to a test question that you took earlier in the day. The brain is linking up current things with memories or knowledge learned in the past.

Energetic Sensitivity

A second type of intuition is called energetic sensitivity. *Energetic sensitivity* is the ability of the nervous system to detect or sense changes in magnetic fields and other types of energies in our environment. These external fields can have a very real effect on us. If we pay attention and our minds are not too noisy, distracted, or cluttered, we can actually sense these energies, either consciously or unconsciously. Let's look at a few examples to illustrate how this works. You may have played with two magnets and felt how they can pull or repel each other. This happens because the magnets radiate what is called a magnetic field or force out into the area around them. The feeling of the pulling or repelling is caused by the magnetic field that surrounds the magnets. In other words, although you can't see the magnetic field, it is real—you can feel the pull. Other examples include cell phones, which use magnetic fields to carry information such as our voice or text messages. Many birds and fish use their ability to detect the earth's magnetic field to know where they are and to get to where they want to go.

We now know that people are also affected by changes in the earth's magnetic field, although most people are normally unaware of it. A good example is that when the earth's magnetic field is disturbed, people may not sleep as well. Disruptions in the earth's magnetic field can also cause us to have more mental fog or lose our self-control and become angry or frustrated more quickly. Some people can sense an earthquake hours or days before it happens. They can sense it before the ground shakes. What they sense are real changes occurring in the earth's magnetic field. (As you will learn in chapter 6, our hearts also create magnetic fields that extend well outside of our bodies!) One final example of energetic sensitivity is the sense that someone is staring at you. Have you ever had that happen? All of these are examples of energetic sensitivity—our ability to sense changes happening outside of us because our nervous system "picks up" or detects the naturally occurring changes in magnetic fields.

Nonlocal Intuition

Another kind of intuition, *nonlocal intuition*, has to do with having a feeling or knowing about something that can't be explained by the other two types of intuition. It has to do, for example, with sensing something about someone who is in another room or even far away, such as in another state or country. It can also be sensing something that may happen in the future. Here are some common examples:

* You sense something is wrong with your cat or dog, and when you get home from school, sure enough, your cat or dog is sick.

* You think about someone you haven't thought of for a while, and all of a sudden you get a text message or phone call from that person.

* You feel like something is about to happen, like a pop quiz or your girlfriend breaking up with you, and then it happens shortly after.

* You sense that someone you care about is in distress or has been injured, and later you find out something did happen. A real example was the mother who all

of a sudden sensed that something happened to her daughter. Her daughter called her a little later and reported that her school bus had had an accident and that she and several other kids were hurt.

Let's look a little more closely at nonlocal intuition and how it can help us with making better choices and decisions that are more aligned with our deeper self. The HeartMath Institute suggests that nonlocal intuition is the wisdom and guidance from one's deeper self, which is an important aspect of our wholeness. Another way of saying this is that intuition is information that comes from our spirit, soul, or however one might speak of or refer to a higher source. When someone talks about having an intuitive insight or a flash of intuition, it is often the wisdom that is coming from our higher source.

Accessing our intuition can help us see a situation in a different, more intelligent way. We're finding that intuition doesn't have to be random or fleeting. As with any new skill, it does take some practice to access our intuition, but we can learn how to do that as well as how to integrate it into our daily lives.

Intuition Research: The Role of the Heart

The scientists at the HeartMath Institute Research Center have learned some fascinating and surprising things about intuition. The HeartMath research clearly shows that the heart plays an important role in intuition, especially nonlocal intuition. Experiments were conducted with people hooked up to different kinds of scientific equipment that measured different aspects of their bodies' functions, including the electrical activity of their brain, heart, and skin. The research showed that the heart appears to pick up on nonlocal intuitive information before the brain does! Although the research was very sophisticated, it can be explained in a simple overview that we think you'll find fascinating. You might find it makes a good topic for a science report!

While hooked up to the research equipment, each participant sat in front of a computer and was instructed simply to watch the screen. The computer randomly showed two different kinds of pictures. One set of pictures was known to evoke calm emotions and included things such as a sunset or a smiling baby. The other set of pictures was known to evoke strong unpleasant feelings and included disgusting, scary things like car accidents, snakes, or angry men. The equipment the participants were hooked up to measured changes that happened in their bodies before, during, and after they looked at the different kinds of pictures. The study concluded that the heart actually tended to know which kind of picture would be shown *before* the computer had even randomly selected a picture and displayed it on the computer screen. The heart, which responded first, then signaled the brain through the nervous system. All of this happened *before* the picture was seen on the computer screen. The research also showed that when people did the Heart Lock-In technique (chapter 6) to get coherent before starting the experiment, their hearts sent a stronger and clearer message to the brain about the type of picture that was going to be shown in the future.

This research suggests that the heart is connected to a deeper source of information. The information from our deeper source isn't just about what kind of picture may come up on a computer screen; it's the wellspring of our heart's intelligence that can act as a moment-to-moment source of practical inner guidance.

Learning how to access your heart's intelligence may not be what you expected to find in a book about stress, but if you really stop to consider what we have talked about, you may very well understand that you have relied on your heart's intuition many times before.

Let's look at the benefits of your heart's intelligence in day-to-day life and how to access that intelligence.

The Role of Intuition in Daily Life

When things just don't seem to be going well and you feel as if you're clunking through the day, you might want to try accessing your intuition. You'll likely find that it can help you flow through day-to-day challenges rather than reacting automatically with impatience or anger, making poor decisions, and not knowing how to handle things that come up. In almost any situation, there are many ways you could respond. Your intuition can give you that inner knowing and self-security of how best to handle an issue. As you gain self-confidence in learning to flow through challenges and make better decisions, you may even find that you can laugh at yourself when you do botch something—and that means less stress. Here's an example:

Have you ever watched an intense game of basketball where Team A sensed they're losing their cool because Team B is "in sync" and is running away with the game and racking up a lot of points? Team A calls a time-out. Why? Because Team A knows several things:

* If they pause for a couple of minutes, they can obtain a clearer perspective of what's happening in the game and come up with a plan to start working together better—more coherently—as a team.

* They can come up with a strategy for making some quick adjustments, hoping to switch the momentum back to their side.

* Taking a time-out can help them recharge their energy.

* They can regain their composure after feeling "victimized" by how well Team B is playing. The coach can encourage them to "go for it." The coach might even say, "Go out there and put your heart into the game."

These same reasons for taking a time-out in the game also apply to your life. That means stepping back from any situation and using your intuition to help you see another way of looking at it.

But what often happens when we get caught up in emotional turmoil and challenging situations is that we drown out our intuition—as Team A did before the time-out. Most of us don't realize that we have the ability to pause and make a shift to where we feel more balanced and composed. It can be as simple as using the Quick Coherence technique (chapter 2) or Attitude Breathing (chapter 4). You can also use the Freeze Frame technique, which we'll explain shortly, to take a deeper look at the situation and ask your heart for intuitive guidance and direction; that's tapping into your heart's intelligence. Especially for issues that gnaw at you, use your heart's intelligence to help you find a calmer, more balanced way—without the emotional ups and downs.

The Freeze Frame Technique

The next technique we're going to share with you is called Freeze Frame. At first as you read the steps, it may sound similar to other stress-reducing techniques you've learned, and it is, but the difference is that it uses the power and intelligence of the heart to help you shift your *perception* of a situation so you can see more possibilities or solutions. That's putting your intuition to work for you. Practicing Freeze Frame doesn't mean all your problems will magically go away. There is no quick fix. Practicing Freeze Frame, however, can help you see that there are other ways of looking at any situation. As a result, you will have more strength, flexibility, common sense, and insight to handle challenging situations or anything that arises.

First, let's see what we mean when we talk about a shift in perception using the following example: We've all heard about natural disasters, such as earthquakes or floods, happening. Perhaps you have even been affected by one. As you might imagine, people can have a wide range of reactions to disasters that are unrelated to how many possessions they lost. Let's say that an area is hit by a devastating earthquake. Afterward, some people move away, determined to never go through such a terrifying experience again. Others seek therapy in hopes of healing the trauma they experienced. However, some who lost their homes and all their belongings adapt quickly and even express appreciation that people in the community came together and worked hard to help each other. They appreciate that they weren't hurt and still have each other. Even though it is the same situation, an earthquake, people *perceive* or see it differently.

While natural disasters are dramatic, any unexpected change or challenge can be very stressful and test your capacity to adapt and be flexible. Your ability to bounce back, pick up the pieces, and move on is directly related to your *perception* of what occurred. Those who recover most quickly and successfully are those who realize that, like it or not, they can't change what happened. Yes, they may have suffered greatly, but they also know that they have to adapt to the new circumstances and move on with life as quickly as possible.

As you learn to access your intuition, you'll be able to change your perception of a situation. Recall the example in chapter 1 where you ripped your favorite jeans on a locker door and then fumed about it. You could choose to keep fuming or you could practice Freeze Frame, which could help you to see that it's really not all that big of a deal and also to remember that your best friend's mother is great at mending clothes. Your heart's intelligence can help you see there are more options than just fuming. That is your heart at work for you, and it helps you decrease the stress in your life.

People often ask where the name "Freeze Frame" came from. When you watch a movie, what you see is a series of still frames or pictures that are moving rapidly. If you push the pause button, you stop or "freeze" the series of pictures so you can see just one frame—hence the name "Freeze Frame." So how does this apply to your daily life? Here's an example:

Maybe you've noticed how quickly life's events can change your moods. You could be walking down the hall at school, feeling angry and upset about the C you got on a science test. Suddenly you run into a good friend who has some great news and all of a sudden you smile, while the moment before, you were feeling low. So it's how you *choose* to respond to each moment in the movie of your life that determines how the next frame unfolds, and eventually how the scene ends. When you mentally or emotionally react to life with frustration, anxiety, indecision, uncertainty, or fear, you drain your energy, produce stress hormones, and keep yourself from getting a clear perspective of the situation—you feel stressed! As a result, your next choice may not be the best one, which can lead to undesirable consequences. Freeze Frame helps you stop your emotional reaction to your "movie" (your situation) by freezing the "frame" (what's happening at the moment) and giving you a time-out to get a clearer perspective on how to respond wisely.

"When a teacher gives a test that seems really unfair and way too hard and I feel myself getting mad, I use Freeze Frame to stop and check it out. By doing Freeze Frame as I'm about to get mad and all bent out of shape, my heart can tell me whether my perception is really true or just there because I'm angry. It's like a reality check. This happened recently with a math test. After doing Freeze Frame, I saw that I really hadn't studied that hard for the test. It was a little hard to see that because part of me wanted to be mad and blame my teacher. Next time, I'll be better prepared for the test."

By using the Freeze Frame technique, you slow your automatic internal reactions and quiet your mind "chatter." By doing so, you are better able to hear the inner promptings of your heart's intelligence and act accordingly.

When to Use Freeze Frame

Practicing Freeze Frame is easier than you may think—and you can use it every day. It's a process that many people do naturally. The intelligence of pausing to take a deeper look before making decisions lies within the heart of each person. You can learn to calm and balance your mind and emotions before making choices in day-to-day life. When you act from a point of balance, you experience increased mental and emotional poise. This eliminates stress and connects you with what your real self would do.

So when exactly can you use the Freeze Frame technique? Here are a few examples:

* when you're not sure how to handle a situation

* when someone puts you down or you feel threatened by someone

* when you feel under a lot of pressure

* when you begin a project and want some creative ideas

* when you're making a decision about something

* when you have to speak your truth to someone and you know that person won't like it

Practicing Freeze Frame is not work; it's something that works for *you*. As you see results, it can become fun. But don't expect miracles or perfection. Skill in using Freeze Frame is developed over time through sincere effort. It's the lack of sincerity that inhibits efforts from reaching their mark, so be genuine when you do it.

Because the Freeze Frame technique is a bit more involved than some of the other techniques you learned, we'll present it a little bit differently. As usual, we'll start out by presenting the technique itself. Read through the steps carefully, but know that you can always come back to this later to refresh your memory of each step. (We also give an abbreviated version called Freeze Frame Quick Steps, which is all you'll need to remember once you get a good feel for practicing it.) Next, as we have done before, we'll list some brief tips to help you get the most out of the Freeze Frame technique. Then we'll give you a worksheet to help you apply the Freeze Frame technique to a situation in your own life.

Technique: Freeze Frame

Step 1: *Acknowledge the problem or issue and any attitudes or feelings about it.*

Step 2: *Focus your attention in the area of the heart. Imagine your breath is flowing in and out of your heart or chest area. Breathe a little slower and deeper than usual.*

Step 3: *Make a sincere attempt to experience a renewing emotion, such as appreciation or care for someone or something in your life.*

Step 4: *From this more objective place, ask yourself what would be a more efficient or effective attitude, action, or solution.*

Step 5: *Quietly observe any subtle changes in perceptions, attitudes, or feelings. Commit to sustaining beneficial attitude shifts and acting on new insights.*

Freeze Frame Quick Steps

Once you understand the steps, you can use these Quick Steps:

1. *Acknowledge the issue and attitudes.*

2. *Do Heart-Focused Breathing.*

3. *Activate a renewing emotion.*

4. *Ask what would be more efficient or effective.*

5. *Observe and act.*

Here are a few helpful tips to get the most out of the Freeze Frame technique:

* Remember that doing the Freeze Frame technique, like doing anything new, requires a sincere effort. As you practice, the technique will begin to feel more natural and the steps will flow more easily.

* Begin practicing Freeze Frame with smaller everyday stressors. Don't start with your biggest stressor or wait for a major crisis to try it! Start smaller so you can get the hang of it. That way you'll gain confidence to use Freeze Frame when bigger problems arise.

Okay, are you ready to give the Freeze Frame technique a try for an issue in your own life? Good! Get started by making a worksheet like the one below in your notebook, or download the worksheet at http://www.newharbinger.com/31946.

Freeze Frame Worksheet

Issue or Situation:

Feelings or Attitudes Before Freeze Frame:

Feelings or Attitudes After Freeze Frame:

Intuition:

Now, before you start the technique itself, take a look at the sample worksheet below. It may give you some ideas about the technique and how to fill out the worksheet as you go through the steps.

Freeze Frame Worksheet—Student Sample

Issue or Situation: *So much homework!*

Feelings or Attitudes Before Freeze Frame: *Overwhelmed, anxious*

Feelings or Attitudes After Freeze Frame: *Calmer, an "I can do" attitude*

Intuition: *Do one thing at a time. Skip some of my computer games this week. I can catch up on the weekend.*

Step by Step: How to Do the Freeze Frame Technique

Now it's time to give Freeze Frame a try. First read each step and the commentary with it. Then go back to the technique section or Quick Steps above and do Freeze Frame beginning with step 1. Take your time with each step. There's no need to rush. Write your responses on the Freeze Frame worksheet in your notebook or on the downloaded worksheet. Have a genuine attitude of fun and exploration as you give the Freeze Frame technique a try!

Step 1: Acknowledge the problem or issue and any attitudes or feelings about it.

Recognizing that you're feeling stressed and acknowledging your attitudes or feelings about problem or issue gives you the opportunity to do something about it.

Step 2: Focus your attention in the area of the heart. Imagine your breath is flowing in and out of your heart or chest area. Breathe a little slower and deeper than usual.

Shifting focus to the heart area helps you stop feeding energy into thinking about the issue and also helps stop an automatic response like frustration or anger. Focusing on your heart and breathing a little slower and deeper is also important in helping you get coherent.

Step 3: Make a sincere attempt to experience a renewing emotion, such as appreciation or care for someone or something in your life.

Remember that it's the *feeling* of the renewing emotion that creates coherence and not just thinking about or visualizing something pleasant.

Step 4: From this more objective place, ask yourself what would be a more efficient or effective attitude, action, or solution.

As you practice this step, keep your focus on the area around your heart as you sincerely ask yourself, *What would be a more efficient or effective attitude, action, or solution?*

Step 5: Quietly observe any subtle changes in perceptions, attitudes, or feelings. Commit to sustaining beneficial attitude shifts and acting on new insights.

In other words, listen to what your heart's intuition is in answer to your question. Remind yourself to stay coherent. Don't go looking for a solution. It's more like letting your intuition "come to you." Be sure to write down in your notebook how you feel about the situation after practicing Freeze Frame as well as any intuitive insight that came to you. Even if it seems that you didn't receive much insight, write down whatever came to you. Intuition often "speaks" quietly.

Sometimes the answers you receive through Freeze Frame can be very simple or might reinforce something you already know. Other times you may experience a "download" of new information and fresh perspectives. At other times, you may not get a clear answer or insight at all. That's okay. It might pop in later, so be open to that. If you get something that doesn't quite make sense to you, then do Freeze Frame around what you got to see if you can get more clarity. To get all the benefit you can from practicing Freeze Frame, be sure to make a genuine effort to follow your heart's intuition.

What's Different About Freeze Frame?

In the past, you may have been told to count to ten or to think positively and just "chill out" if you got angry about something. Counting to ten may help cool you down for a moment, but it doesn't necessarily change your *perception* of the situation or person. For example, if you're angry about something a friend did and you count to ten to chill out about it, it doesn't mean you're not still upset and stewing about it. Chances are, by the count of eleven, you're reengaged and caught back up in the same emotional turmoil. To change your perception means to change the way you look at the situation. That's the only way to find effective, lasting solutions. Keep in mind that the amount of stress you feel is based on your perception of a person, situation, or event.

***

Now that you've learned about intuition and how you can access it by using the Freeze Frame technique, you'll be able to use the insights you get to help you navigate your daily life with a lot less stress. Next, we're going to talk about how you can learn to relate better with others. It may be a slightly different way of relating with others than you have been taught in the past. We're also going to share some science that we bet you'll find interesting—your invisible connection with others.

Your Stress-Bustin', Resilience-Boostin', On-the-Go Action Plan

1. Do the Freeze Frame technique at least two times each day for the next week.

2. Try doing the Freeze Frame technique on the go.

chapter 6

Invisible Communication
The Unseen Effect of Emotions and Attitudes

When we talk about communicating with or relating to others, we usually think about doing this with words, body language, and tone of voice. In this chapter, however, we're going to talk about some surprising "invisible" ways that people relate to and communicate with each other. This "invisible communication" may not be something that your textbooks talk about, but it's very real and it happens all the time! You experience it yourself every day without even knowing it. Although it's invisible, you can sure feel it. And as you might have guessed by now, your heart plays an important and fascinating role in this kind of communication. Let's take a look now at this "invisible communication."

Feelings in the Air

Have you ever walked into a room, and even though no one was saying anything, you could feel tension in the air? You couldn't quite explain how you had the feeling, but you could sense that an argument or disagreement had just taken place. Something just felt "off." There is even an expression that describes this sensation: "The tension was so thick that you could cut it with a knife."

Or maybe you have felt tension, dread, or anxiety in your classroom on the day of a big test or when a pop quiz was announced. The air felt "heavy." Perhaps when your mother got home from work, you could tell the moment she walked in the door that she had had a rotten day. It was just a feeling you had that let you know that it was not the best of days. Or maybe you've come home having had a rotten day, and even though you didn't say anything, your family could just sense you'd had a bad day.

On the other hand, have you noticed there are some people who make you feel good just to be around them? Maybe you walk into one of your classes or sit down with some friends and you feel uplifted. Something just feels good. Or perhaps you have felt the "excitement in the air" around a special holiday, sporting event, or other fun event. So just what is it that's happening that makes it possible for you to sense those types of things?

The Electricity of the Heart

To help understand this, we're going to give you another short science lesson about your heart. It turns out your heart can play a big role in this invisible communication. We think you'll find it pretty fascinating stuff.

Earlier we talked about how the different emotions you experience create different heart rhythm patterns—depleting emotions create an incoherent heart rhythm and renewing emotions create a more coherent heart rhythm. Now let's look at another amazing fact about the heart.

Every time your heart beats, it actually produces electricity. There is a device called an electrocardiograph that doctors use in their offices to measure the electricity produced by a person's heart. Doctors use an electrocardiograph to check for problems with the electrical activity of the heart. Typically, the way it works is that a nurse puts electrodes on a person's chest to pick up the heart's electrical signals so they can be measured. Doctors in some hospitals use a device called a superconducting quantum interference device to measure the heart's magnetic field. How's that for a mouthful! Good thing it's commonly referred to as a SQUID. Looking at the heart's magnetic field can help doctors find the source of a problem in someone's heart.

Whenever electricity is produced, a magnetic field is also produced. A magnetic field is measured with a device called a *magnetometer*, and a SQUID is just a special type of magnetometer. Together, the electricity and the magnetic field are called an *electromagnetic field*. We're going to call it a magnetic field to make it simpler. Don't worry about the long words. What's important is what we're going to explain next.

What's interesting about magnetic fields is that they go *through* things such as walls, doors, cars, school buses—they go through about *everything!* Magnetic fields not only go through things, but they also carry information. Because a magnetic field can go through things, that's what makes it possible for cell phones, for example, to be able to work when you're inside a building. It's what makes it possible for a car radio to work. In the case of cell phones, the information the magnetic field carries is text and voice messages, and the photos you send from one cell phone to another. In the case of a radio in a car, it's the magnetic field that carries or broadcasts the music playing at the radio station to your car's radio.

So what do cell phones and your heart have in common? Now that's an interesting question! If a magnetic field carries or broadcasts your cell phone information (that is, your voice and text messages), then what does the magnetic field radiating from your heart carry? Here's a hint: It's something we've been talking a whole lot about. You can think of the magnetic field produced by your heart as carrying or broadcasting your emotions.

Remember that we said that magnetic fields go through things? The magnetic field your heart produces goes through your body and even the clothes you're wearing—no matter how many layers of sweaters, coats, and long underwear you have on. Your heart's magnetic field can actually be measured three feet away from your body using a magnetometer. It's believed that it goes much farther than three feet, but the equipment that scientists have now is not sensitive enough to measure it farther. (By the way, the magnetic field is not the same thing as an aura, which is perhaps a term you've heard some people use.)

The Heart's Magnetic Field

Take a look at the diagram below. The diagram was made by a computer to show the shape of the heart's magnetic field. The diagram is a good way to see that the magnetic field extends out beyond your body in all directions—front, back, sideways, and head to toe. What else do you notice about the magnetic fields? Take a close look. They overlap and cross over each other. Think for a moment what that might mean.

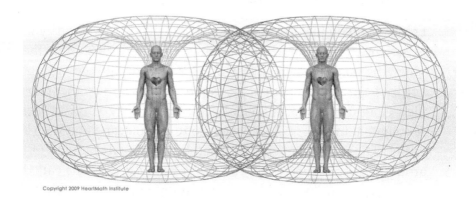

Copyright 2009 HeartMath Institute

Your emotions and attitudes, all of them, are being carried or broadcast by your heart's magnetic field out beyond your body and are mixing with other people's magnetic fields. And their magnetic fields are bumping into yours! You can think of this as a type of *energetic communication*. It can help explain why being around someone who is anxious or angry, for example, doesn't feel very good. In a very real sense, they are sending out that anxious or angry feeling by their magnetic field and you can feel it. If you are frustrated or bothered about something or have a lousy attitude, others can feel that, if they are sensitive or paying attention, because that's what you're sending out. So we are all affecting each other all the time with our emotions— whether or not we are aware of it. Of course, feelings of care, excitement, joy, enthusiasm, and calm, for instance, are also carried by your magnetic field. That can explain why it feels good to be around certain people; you can feel their renewing emotions.

Feeding the Field

From what you just learned, you can see that the emotions you experience throughout the day—the depleting ones and the renewing ones—don't just stay inside you. They go out around you and can affect other people in the same way that other people's emotions and attitudes affect you. It's why you can feel "excitement in the air" or "tension so thick you can cut it with a knife." The magnetic field produced by your heart radiates out around you and surrounds you, forming what could be called your very own "personal field environment." Now let's go a step further. You can think of your emotions, then, as what you are "feeding the field." Remember, just like the diagram above shows, the magnetic field is all around you and can potentially be felt by other people.

In earlier chapters, you began taking an inventory of the emotions you experience each day, both those that drain your inner battery and that feel really lousy and those that revitalize you. Now that you know you are "feeding the field" with your emotions and that others can feel them whether or not they are aware of it, you might ask yourself, *What am I feeding the field?* In other words, *Am I radiating or broadcasting depleting emotions that may drag others down, or am I radiating renewing emotions that might just give a friend a boost?*

On the flip side, you can often sense when something feels off about your friends—they just don't seem like themselves. They may look fine, say they're fine, but maybe you detect they're worried about something or are unusually self-absorbed. You may be right. So rather than automatically giving someone a hard time or taking it personally when you sense things are out of sync, take a moment to consider that there might be an emotion running beneath the radar. Getting into your heart can help you find patience and understanding.

Getting coherent, then, is important because you can change what you're feeding the field. Getting coherent, in other words, helps you hold steady when others are upset or not quite themselves. It helps you to be flexible and stay balanced so you don't get pulled into any drama. Responding with more drama to someone else's drama doesn't help you, the other person, or the situation.

By asking yourself what you are feeding the field, you are taking a big step in being responsible—not only for yourself, but also for how you impact others. That's important self-awareness. Being self-responsible takes maturity. Being self-responsible helps your maturity grow. So make it fun by asking yourself throughout the day, *What am I feeding the field right now?*

Another way to think of it is that whatever feeling you are radiating outward, you are surrounding yourself in it, too. So, for example, not only do you feel anxious inside, but you're also surrounded by that anxious feeling. And who wants to be surrounded by a feeling like that? Why not surround yourself with a field environment that's filled with "good vibes"?

How We Can Affect Others

We're going to describe an interesting experiment that tried to determine if people could affect others when they are coherent. In this experiment, forty people were divided into ten groups with four people in each group.

Benefits of a Coherent Field Environment

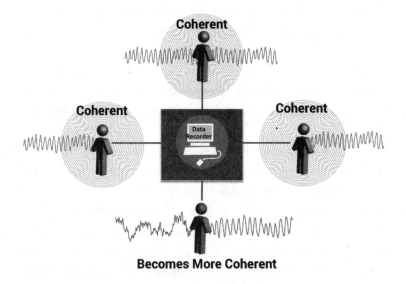

Becomes More Coherent

Three of the four people in each group were taught how to get coherent by practicing Quick Coherence (chapter 2). They practiced it for only a couple of weeks. Each group of four people sat around a table with each person hooked up to a device that measured their heart rhythms. The three people

120

who were taught how to get coherent were instructed to practice the technique as they sat there. The fourth person did not know the others were doing anything other than just sitting around the table. What do you suppose happened to the fourth person when the other three got coherent? If you guessed that the fourth person became more coherent, you're right. As the three people got more in sync, their heart rhythms shifted into a smooth and ordered pattern. What the researchers found really interesting was that the fourth person's heart rhythms also became more coherent. The experiment showed that we can indeed affect others by our personal field environments and the emotions we experience.

Next is a fun experiment that includes two graphs showing how the heart rhythms change when one gets coherent and how it measurably affects another.

Josh and Mabel, His Dog

In this next experiment, you'll see that it's not just people that can be affected by other people's emotions—animals can, too. Josh's dad is a scientist at the HeartMath Institute Research Center. One day when Josh was twelve, his dad asked him to come to the research lab and told him to bring his dog, Mabel. His dad put a noninvasive heart rhythm monitor on both Josh and Mabel so that he could measure the activity happening in Josh and Mabel's hearts. The following graph shows what happened. We'll explain the experiment so you'll understand what you see in the graphs.

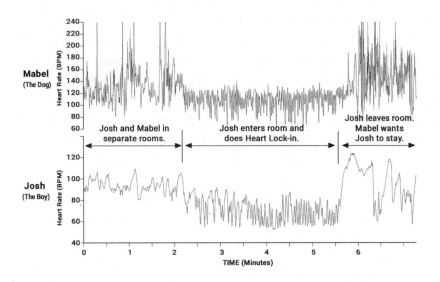

Looking at the diagram, you'll see that the top graph shows Mabel's heart rhythms and the bottom graph shows Josh's heart rhythms. At the top left, you'll see the graph labeled "Josh and Mabel in separate rooms," which is when the experiment started. Mabel was in the lab sniffing around while Josh was in another room. You can see that Mabel's heart rhythm pattern is chaotic. Josh's heart rhythms were also incoherent.

Josh's dad then told Josh to go into the lab where Mabel was, sit down, and not touch or talk to Mabel. Josh then did a HeartMath technique called the Heart Lock-In, which we will teach you shortly. Basically, Josh sent love and appreciation to Mabel for several minutes. Notice what happened to Josh's heart rhythms when he practiced the technique. His heart rhythms became smoother, or what you now know is called a coherent heart rhythm. Look at what happened to Mabel's heart rhythms when Josh became coherent. Her heart rhythms became coherent, too! Their coherent heart rhythms are shown in the middle part of the two graphs. Remember, Josh was not touching her or talking to her. Finally, Josh was told to get up and leave the room, leaving Mabel by herself. You can see how both of their heart rhythms then became incoherent.

More studies have been done to show how one's emotions can affect other people, but this was a fun way to show that we can affect others, even animals. When Josh did the Heart Lock-In technique, he activated the feeling of love and "sent" it to Mabel. What was really happening was that the feeling of love was being carried on his magnetic field. Mabel could feel it and she became coherent, too.

Ellen and Tonopah, Her Horse

Another simple study took place in a corral rather than in a lab. Professor Ellen Gehrke has a number of horses and was curious to see if her coherence could affect her horses in the same way Mabel became coherent when Josh got coherent.

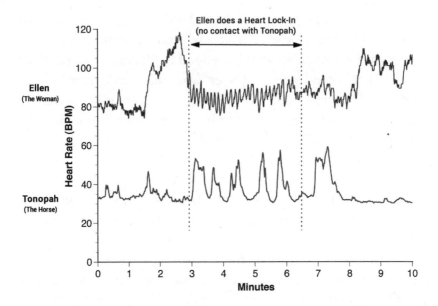

One of the researchers went to Dr. Gehrke's farm and hooked her up to a heart rhythm monitor. She also hooked up each of the horses to a monitor, one at a time. Ellen walked into the corral and sat down near one of the horses. She did not touch or speak to the horse. She did a Heart Lock-In, and just as Mabel became coherent as Josh got coherent, the horse became coherent, too. You can see in the above graph how the heart rhythms of each changed into a more coherent pattern. The researcher hooked up four of the horses to heart rhythm monitors and got the same results for all but one. The one that did not become coherent is well known for not liking humans.

After the study, Dr. Gehrke talked about horses: "Horses receive information from body language and give feedback. They don't think very much, they *feel*. They are very emotional and honest. They also have a powerful impact on your sense of self and ability to lead."

Heart Lock-In Technique

Now we want to introduce the Heart Lock-In technique to you. It's a favorite of many people. For one, it feels good practicing it. And if you practice it regularly, you may begin to feel better more often and you may also become more resilient—from the inside out. It helps you add more coherence into your system so that the coherent state becomes more familiar and automatic.

The Heart Lock-In is a coherence-building technique because it requires you to activate or experience a renewing emotion, similar to the Quick Coherence technique (chapter 2), but for a longer period of time. It's a powerful technique that you can use whenever you want to go deeper into your heart. Using this technique can be a refreshing break from all your busy head thoughts. With a little practice, it activates your heart coherence, helping you maintain more inner balance during your busy day. Also, with practice, the Heart Lock-In can release feelings of insecurity, anger, anxiety, and other depleting emotions. As you get more coherent, the old attitudes and emotional reactions release bit by bit.

First, we'll introduce the three steps of the technique. Next, we'll give you some helpful tips to get the most out of the Heart Lock-In. Then we will explain each step in more depth before you give it a try.

"The Heart Lock-In is one of the best things to help me deal with my stress. I can leave behind all the school pressures and get calmer. It is kind of like taking a shower. I wash away all the dirt."

Technique: Heart Lock-In

Step 1: *Focus your attention in the area of the heart. Imagine your breath is flowing in and out of your heart or chest area, breathing a little slower and deeper than usual.*

Step 2: *Activate and sustain a renewing feeling such as appreciation, care, or compassion.*

Step 3: *Radiate that renewing feeling to yourself and others.*

Here are a few helpful tips to get the most out of the Heart Lock-In:

* If distracting thoughts come up (for example, worry about an upcoming test or excitement about the party tomorrow night), acknowledge them and then, as quickly as possible, refocus on your heart and breathe a little slower and deeper.

* Be patient with yourself. For many, it takes regular practice to get comfortable using this technique. Patience goes a long way!

* If you are having a bad day, don't abandon the Heart Lock-In practice. This might be the best time to do it!

Step by Step: How to Do the Heart Lock-In Technique

Step 1: Focus your attention in the area of the heart. Imagine your breath is flowing in and out of your heart or chest area, breathing a little slower and deeper than usual.

You probably recognize this step as the Heart-Focused Breathing technique (chapter 1). Hopefully, you've been doing Heart-Focused Breathing a lot throughout your day. Remember, you can do it anytime, anywhere, and no one knows you're doing it.

Step 2: Activate and sustain a renewing feeling such as appreciation, care, or compassion.

This step is similar to step 2 in the Quick Coherence technique (chapter 2). In both techniques, you activate a renewing feeling. In the Heart Lock-In technique, after you activate a renewing feeling, you sustain it. You might think of sustaining a renewing feeling as "locking into it" and "holding on to it"—"it" being the renewing feeling. Who wouldn't want to lock in and hang out in a renewing feeling? When you first start practicing Heart Lock-In, generate the feeling of appreciation or care by choosing something that's easy for you to appreciate or care about—such as a special friendship; your dog or cat; a warm coat for a cold, wintry day; a teacher who spent some extra time to help you sort out a problem; or the sun shining after days of rain.

Step 3: Radiate that renewing feeling to yourself and others.

Then in this step, you radiate or send out the renewing feeling. You don't have to push it out or force anything to happen here. It's enough to have the intent to radiate the renewing feeling. Having the intent is like giving yourself instructions and then just letting it happen. Some people have found it helpful to think of waves radiating out like the ripples that go out when you throw a stone in the water. Others think of the image of the sun radiating out warmth. In step 3, you're "giving off" or "sending out" a renewing emotion in a similar way. Appreciation or care is a great feeling to feed the field!

Before you begin, decide what renewing feeling you would like to activate. When you get to steps 2 and 3, take your time. We want you to hang out in the feeling for at least two minutes to begin with, or three minutes if you can stretch yourself. Why? Because not only does it feel good to do so, but by staying coherent longer, you naturally build coherence into your body. When that happens, you might start to notice that things that once troubled you don't bother you anymore—or at least not nearly as much. You might notice—or others might notice—that you are calmer, even when you're not practicing a technique. The more coherence you build, the more naturally resilient you'll be. One more thing: we suggest that you find a quiet place to practice the Heart Lock-In, and close your eyes as you do it.

You can do a Heart Lock-In for as long as you like, but do it now for about two or three minutes or longer. After you practice it, write down in your notebook what you observed or noticed as you did it. Maybe you'll decide to do it again. Great! Do it often.

A Few More Helpful Hints

Now that you have done your first Heart Lock-In, let's check in. Perhaps you noticed that your mind was really active at times and was wandering all over the place. This is normal, especially when you are first learning it, but it happens to more experienced people, too. For instance, during your first few times trying out Heart Lock-In, you may find yourself thinking about some fun future event or even worrying about an upcoming school project. When these thoughts come up, acknowledge them, refocus your attention on your heart, and breathe a little slower and deeper. Even though your focus will be challenged and you might drift in and out of practicing the technique, the fact that you are doing it at all is *big*.

Keep expanding the length of time you do the Heart Lock-In technique. See if you can go from a two- to three-minute lock-in to five minutes at the end of the week. And above all, be patient with yourself.

When to Do a Heart Lock-In

Practice the Heart Lock-In technique in a quiet place for three to fifteen minutes, one or more times a day, to build your power to sustain coherence. You might want to first do it for three to five minutes and gradually, as you get more familiar with it, do it for longer periods. You might find you want to do it for thirty minutes. Great! An effective time to practice a Heart Lock-In is at the beginning of your day. It's a great way to kick off your day by activating a renewing feeling and soaking yourself in that good feeling. Radiate the renewing feeling to your entire day or to a friend. Or just simply radiate it out. You might also practice it during a midafternoon break in order to get coherent and add energy to your battery.

Another good time to the Heart Lock-In is before you go to bed or when you feel like crashing because you're worn out. Many people find it helps them fall asleep faster or sleep deeper. Better sleep helps recharge your inner battery. With a fully charged inner battery, you have greater ability to handle any of life's situations.

There are other times, too, that you might want to do a Heart Lock-In. Sometimes it can be helpful to radiate care to yourself when you're in a tough situation, such as before a test or maybe when you're sick. In fact, you could activate any of the replacement attitudes listed in chapter 4 and radiate those to yourself and to others. You could also radiate a renewing feeling to a friend who's having a difficult time. When you get the hang of doing it, you'll know just the right time to use the Heart Lock-In.

✳✳✳

You can see now that how you feel inside—calm, patient, angry, bored, sad, or happy, for instance—not only affects you, but those emotions and attitudes also can affect other people. Others can sense your frustration, and they can feel your care and appreciation, too. Practicing the Heart Lock-In technique is a powerful way to generate more coherence in your system and charge your battery while also "feeding the field" around you with renewing emotions that can help uplift and support others.

In the next chapter, you'll see that how you feel inside also affects how you communicate with others. Communication, as it turns out, is a major source of stress, and considering we're communicating with each other every day, it's well worth exploring. We'll also talk about something you're probably quite familiar with—drama—but we'll look at it with a twist.

Your Stress-Bustin', Resilience-Boostin' On-the-Go Action Plan

1. As always, continue to notice when you're draining your inner battery. It's not unusual for small energy drains to sneak up and before you know it, the situation or issue becomes a big energy drain. Catch them early! Use your notebook and write down energy drains.

2. Throughout the day, ask yourself, *Which quadrant of the Emotional Landscape am I in right now? In which quadrant would I like to be? What technique will I practice to help get me there?* Have fun doing this. If you keep using the Landscape (chapter 3) and the techniques, we think you'll find that you are spending more time on the right side of the Landscape. You may find it gets a little easier to make the inner shift to feeling balanced and calmer.

3. Practice the Heart Lock-In technique at least once a day for the next week. Do it for at least three to five minutes each time. You might want to do it longer—maybe ten or fifteen minutes! Eventually, you might find you want to do it even longer. Write down in your notebook what you observe when you do it. You might also write down when you feel it would be most helpful for you to do it.

chapter 7

Coherent Communication
Taking the Stress Out

You may be wondering why there's a chapter on communication in a book about stress. You might also be considering skipping this chapter because communication sounds pretty boring. But hang on and don't flip the pages to the next chapter or close the book! Communication turns out to be a hot topic because it's one of the biggest sources of stress. You get along with some people, but others drive you crazy. You can talk to some people, but with others it's more difficult. The quality of your communication plays a major role in how well you navigate through your daily interactions with peers, friends, teachers, family, and even strangers.

Communicating well sounds easy enough, but all too often teens—and adults—end up making a big mess of it. Because you communicate every single day in many different ways, it's worth trying to get better at it. When you can communicate well, not only will your life be less stressful, it will also be more interesting and fun!

"My parents are really busy and stressed out. They don't listen when I talk. For right now, we just tune each other out."

"I avoid certain people and groups at my school. We are on different wavelengths. There is no point trying to talk to them. They're all idiots."

"Talking to some kids at school is like talking to a zombie. Nothing comes back."

"My parents put a lot of pressure on me to get good grades, but then they hardly pay attention to all the other stuff that is going on. It is really frustrating to be around them sometimes."

Over the next few pages, we're going to offer several ways to improve communication. Let's start by looking at some of the basic ways we communicate every day.

Everyday Communication

It's almost impossible to go anywhere or do anything without communicating with other people. Talking is the main way you share information, ideas, stories, points of view, likes/dislikes, or the cool new app you just found.

Obviously, the main way you communicate is through words. Your words might describe a fun time you had with a friend. You also use words to explain something you just learned, to ask a question, or to talk with someone about a difficult situation in your life.

Words are not only spoken, but they are also written. You probably communicate a lot during the day with written words through text messages, e-mails, or answering questions on a test or writing a paper for a class. You read them in magazines and on signs, too. Written words are everywhere.

So now that we've talked about how we communicate through words (spoken or written), let's explore communication in a way that might be a little different than what you've learned—a way, however, that can help you make the most of what you have already learned about communication. How well you communicate can make a big difference in getting along with people and how you handle social situations—and how much stress you have. And once again, your heart and emotions are, shall we say, at the heart of good communication—both as a speaker and a listener.

Communicating is a Two-Way Street

Let's look first at a couple of basics of communication. Although quite obvious, communication is between a speaker and a listener. And good communication begins when you are more emotionally balanced. With more ability to self-regulate and take charge of your emotions, you can speak with more sincerity and are better able to carefully choose your words, which can make a big difference between blurting something out and saying it with care. Being emotionally balanced helps keep communication clear so you aren't sending mixed messages where you say one thing, but you're thinking or feeling very differently.

Speak from Your Heart: Honest Communication

As we said a moment ago, communication is a two-way street; it involves a speaker and a listener. When you are the speaker, in order to communicate well, it's important to *speak from your heart*, which means being emotionally balanced and centered and being honest about your thoughts and feelings. To speak from the heart, you first take a moment to get clear on how you truly feel about an issue and the main point of what you want to say. You begin by being honest with yourself, and to do so, it's important to make sure that what you say matches with how you feel and what you think. If what you say does not match up with how you feel and what you think, you can end up sending mixed messages—and that can really mess up communication.

When speaking from your heart, however, it is *very* important to keep in mind that if you want to truly be heard by others, it is not helpful or smart to yell and scream at them. Sometimes you may need to speak in a firm tone, but exploding will only trigger emotional reactions and will put your listener on the defensive. And when you're in a defensive mode, you really can't hear what someone else has to say. As best as possible, try and get coherent first before communicating. In some cases, you might feel upset or emotional, but try to find a place of greater self-control and speak from there. Speak in a way that you would like to be spoken to, and also be open to hearing feedback from others without reacting negatively.

Sometimes it's appropriate to "speak your truth"—that is, honestly communicate your feelings and thoughts about a situation. For example, someone at school might try to get you to take drugs and you don't want to. Speaking your truth might be saying just that—that you simply don't want to, even knowing that others may sneer at you and think you're a wimp if you don't take drugs like they do. Speaking your truth, which is speaking with the honesty of your heart, is often one of the last things people will do out of fear of the other person's response.

Recall a time when you were afraid to speak your truth. How did you feel? Chances are it got all bottled up inside you, and you carried that burden for days, maybe even weeks. That's a good time to ask yourself, *Which is the better choice—living with the discomfort from bottling everything up inside or finding the courage to speak my deeper truth?* Sometimes you may need a third person—someone more neutral—to talk with or have with you when you need to communicate with someone concerning a big issue. With most everyday relationships, though, just try to find the courage to say what you mean and mean what you say, but do it from a place of inner balance and calm.

We can always find reasons for not speaking from our heart, and in the moment, those reasons may feel justified. But are they really? Do any of these reasons for not speaking from your heart ever apply to you?

* I already know what they're going to say.

* They never listen. Why would it be different this time?

* It won't change anything anyway.

* I'm hoping the problem will just go away.

* They might judge me for saying what I feel.

* They won't understand.

* I don't want them to think I'm rude.

* I'm not really clear, so I'll wait until I am.

* I should be past this.

* It will just turn into an argument.

* I might say it all wrong.

* I'm waiting for the right time to speak.

* If I share my truth, I can't trust that it will be confidential.

Do any of those sound familiar? It's very easy for your head to come in with all kinds of reasons not to speak from your heart. But are they really in your best interest?

Recall a recent situation that became more stressful because you were hesitant to say how you really felt. Could it have played out differently if you had communicated how you really felt? Perhaps speaking up might have helped relieve some of the stress you were feeling. When you do this, the other person may not agree with you or may not be able to really understand, but you will know you are genuine. You're being true to yourself. That's worth a lot. Speaking from your heart can feel good and give you the confidence to do it again. You might just be surprised with the results! Remember to speak the way you would like to be spoken to. It will help the listener hear what it is you are saying.

We have been talking about speaking skills, but that's only one part of communication. Let's look next at the importance of learning to listen well and the benefits that you can gain from doing that.

Deep Heart Listening

Deep heart listening means to sincerely listen to and hear what another person says. It does not mean you have to agree with what the person says, nor does that person have to agree with what you say. Deep heart listening helps you get a better sense of what someone is *really* saying so you can understand where the person is coming from and how the person feels. It helps you hear what's *behind* the words, which is sometimes called the "essence" of what the person says. It can help create a deeper connection with the person, too. Deep heart listening is also a way of respecting others because it lets them know you are willing to listen to their point of view, while at the same time it helps you to understand them and where they're coming from. As you listen deeply, you help others feel genuinely heard and cared for.

Being a good listener is an important part of communication; it's half of that two-way street that we talked about earlier. If a person feels like you have really listened, he or she will be a lot more open to hearing what you have to say. It makes for a much better conversation, and having these kinds of conversations can be some of the most fulfilling moments in life—both as a teen and also later on as an adult. The payoffs are huge if you really work at good communication!

When Are You Deep Heart Listening?

So how do you deep heart listen? You start with getting coherent and genuinely hearing not only the words people say, but also the deeper meaning behind their words.

To help you know when (or if) you're deep heart listening, think about people you turn to for real support and under-standing; chances are they are good listeners. When you talk with good listeners, you may have conversations that are more genuine. Are there certain friends or adults you can turn to when you have a problem or need to be listened to? What is their listening like?

* Are they compassionate and understanding?

* Are they totally present, giving you their full attention?

* Do they try to solve your problems for you, or do they help you to get your own clarity so you can find the best solutions for situations?

* Do they let you talk until you've finished saying what you want to say?

* And their body language—do they maintain eye contact, lean in, nod occasionally?

You can develop these same qualities and when you do, you will be less likely to take sides in an issue or get pulled into drama. Your friends will more likely feel that they've been heard.

When Are You Not Deep Heart Listening?

How do you know if you're *not* deep heart listening? Here are some clues:

* Do you interrupt or finish other people's sentences for them?

* Do you try to figure out what they are going to say next?

* Are you busy solving their problems for them while they're talking?

* Do you try to convince them they should feel a different way?

* Are you giving partial attention to the person because you're distracted by something else?

If you answered yes to any of the above questions, chances are that you are not practicing deep heart listening. And if others answer yes to any of those questions, they aren't deep heart listening either. To illustrate, let's say you are telling a friend about the lousy day you had and you describe all the things that happened. Your friend, however, is texting someone else during your conversation and she keeps asking you to repeat what you said. She certainly is not deep heart listening. Deep heart listening means that she puts the phone down and genuinely pays attention, without distractions, to what you are saying. She might ask questions or acknowledge that a lot of lousy stuff did happen to you today. In the second scenario (when she listens), you are likely to feel that you have been heard. It might not solve all the problems, but feeling heard is worth a lot.

We've talked about the importance of being a good speaker—speaking from your heart—and a good listener—doing deep heart listening. The next technique, Coherent Communication, can help you gain the ability to be both a better speaker and listener, which is at the heart of good communication.

Technique: Coherent Communication

The Coherent Communication technique can help you be both a better speaker and a better listener. To learn the technique, we'll give the steps first, followed by the Quick Steps, which you can use to refresh your memory of how to do the technique. Next, we'll give you some helpful tips, and after that, we'll walk you through the steps and give a little more detail.

Coherent Communication Technique

Step 1: *Get coherent before communicating in order to effectively share and receive information.*

Step 2: *Listen for the essence of what is being said without prejudging or getting pulled into drama before the communication is complete. Speak in a genuine tone and consider what you are going to say in response and how it may impact others.*

Step 3: *During important or sensitive communications, confirm the essence of what you heard to ensure mutual understanding.*

Coherent Communication Quick Steps

Once you understand the steps, you can use these Quick Steps:

1. *Shift into heart coherence.*

2. *Listen for the essence; speak with a genuine tone.*

3. *Confirm mutual understanding.*

Here are a few helpful tips to get the most out of the Coherent Communication technique:

* Before you begin, set an intention to be respectful of others' views or situations.

* Remember to recenter in your heart if you start to overreact or lose emotional composure.

Step by Step: How to Do the Coherent Communication Technique

Step 1: Get coherent before communicating in order to effectively share and receive information.

Use Heart-Focused Breathing (chapter 1), Quick Coherence (chapter 2), or Attitude Breathing (chapter 4) to get coherent. Don't rush this step. Practice Quick Coherence or Attitude Breathing with your eyes *open* so that when you're talking with people, you can get coherent and they won't even notice. In the middle of a conversation, it's okay to tell them you want to pause for a moment. That's honest communication, too!

Step 2: Listen for the essence of what is being said without pre-judging and getting pulled into drama before the communication is complete. Speak from a genuine tone and consider what you are going to say in response and how it may impact others.

When you listen for the essence, you're listening for the deeper meaning of what the person is saying. A friend may tell you everything is okay and nothing is bothering him, but when you listen for the essence, you may detect that he is worried about something. You're also simply listening, without all sorts of other thoughts or judgments running in your head.

Step 3: During important or sensitive communications, confirm the essence of what you heard to ensure mutual understanding.

Confirm what you heard to be certain you've understood what the speaker was saying. Because we're often in a rush, this is the step most of us forget.

When you confirm understanding, you can just say a few words or a few sentences. It is not necessary to repeat the person's entire message. When the other person feels as if you truly understand, it is at that level where true confirmation takes place—it's more than just the words. For example, your teacher gives your class detailed instructions about an upcoming assignment and goes over two pages of instructions that you will need to follow. To confirm the essence of what you heard, you might say something like this: "So to get started, we should read all the instructions again, but by next Tuesday, you only want us to have the first four items complete. And if we have questions about anything, we can just ask you. Is that right?" If it is correct, your teacher will say so, or if he wants you to do the first *five* items by next Tuesday, he can clarify that for the class. After all, he might have said the first four items but actually meant the first five.

Of course it's not practical to confirm mutual understanding in everyday casual conversation, but in important communications, it can save a lot of misunderstandings and miscommunications—and therefore it can also save a lot of stress.

Challenges to Coherent Communication

Now that you've learned what coherent communication is, let's take a look at some of the places where you may run into challenges. Applying what you've learned might just help improve your communication so you can handle these challenges better.

A Gap in Communication: Not Feeling Understood

As a teen, you may feel that you are frequently misunderstood—not only by your parents and teachers, but also by your peers who may label you as a jock, nerd, hipster, geek, or prep. That can cause a lot of stress. For sure, adults do have a hard time understanding teens. They get really busy and, in a knee-jerk kind of way, will tell you in absolute terms what to do and how to behave without truly understanding you and your situation. Or because they are older, they always feel they know best and may think your opinions are wrong or immature. For some of you, it may often seem there is no time or space to talk with your parents. Practicing the Coherent Communication technique or Attitude Breathing (chapter 4) can help offset this communication gap. If you don't get the results you hope for the first time you practice a technique, try it again later. You'll build your confidence and your ability to navigate challenging situations.

Communicating with Your Parents

The transformations you are undergoing can dramatically affect the quality of your communication with your parents. There can be a real gap in understanding each other. Some of you may get the standard, passed-down recipes for life from your parents, and you write your parents off as not really understanding you. And, in fact, that is sometimes the case; they really don't understand you. Many of your parents and other adults in the family are trying to either adjust to the changes they see in you, or they treat you like the child you were three or four years ago. They may misread your moods, overreact to your misbehavior or rule breaking, expect good grades without knowing your full schedule, frequently point out only the negative stuff, and just not spend enough quality time with you. In short, many parents really don't know how to adjust while others are unwilling to adjust to the changes you are going through. This can create friction and a lot of stress!

Because of the transformation and stresses you go through as a teen, you often need more sensitivity and understanding from adults due to the extra amped-up emotions you sometimes have. Parents and teachers could help more if they let teens know that they can't always understand them, even if they're really trying. And, because they can't, it's sometimes hard for teens to respect the useful trial-and-error knowledge their parents have.

As a teen, you need to do your part, too, which begins with understanding and acknowledging your moods, attitudes, and behaviors that can also widen the communication gap. Here's a look at how that can happen.

You've probably heard adults say, "I wish I had known that when I was your age." And many adults really do wish they had known what they know now as an adult when they were teens. Teens ignore a lot of things adults have learned that got them through difficult times in their lives. When you're a teen, coming into your own sense of yourself, you feel right about your perceptions and feel like you know what you know. Current times are not the same as when your parents were teens. But adults sometimes have strong convictions about what is right because of the knowledge they have gained from trial and error. This wisdom might actually be a shortcut to help you work out a situation. Sometimes, the truth of who is right is somewhere in between. Both teens and adults have good points and can learn from one another when they respect each other. That mutual respect doesn't happen as much as it should because parents and teens simply don't understand each other.

Here's a common example of a breakdown in communication. A sixteen-year-old wants to go to a big party. Everyone is going to be there. She wants to drive her parents' car and pick up a couple of friends on the way. Because she just got her driver's license, her parents don't feel she's ready to drive at night, especially with other kids in the car. She doesn't believe it will be a problem and doesn't pick up on or honor her parents' concerns for her safety. Instead, she gets angry that her parents won't let her drive the family car. She locks herself away in her room, depressed and angry for hours. Underneath the emotional meltdown, however, if she could push the pause button on her emotional response—by practicing Heart-Focused Breathing (chapter 1), for instance—she might sense that they are right or she may at least have a respectful understanding of why they are saying no even though she may not be happy about it. Maybe her parents have learned from their own trial-and-error experiences the dangers of driving home from a party under the possible influence of alcohol. The daughter may never admit to such a possibility, but her parents are not naïve to the many risks associated with teen behavior. After all, they were once teens, too. But because the daughter doesn't feel understood in other areas of their communication, she can't hear or respect her parents in this one issue.

What we just described may not be your exact situation, but you can probably think of examples that fit your experience. So what can teens do? They can try to understand that it's not that some adults *won't* understand, it's simply that they *can't* understand. Just knowing that can cut out a lot of hurt, pain, and depression. It's not that many of your parents don't love and care about you, but sometimes they don't know *how* to show the love they have.

Let's look at another example of how miscommunication can play out and also how to use the Coherent Communication technique to turn it around. Here's what it might sound like when a parent misreads your moods:

Parent: I'm really tired of your bad attitude lately. It's dragging me down, and I've got so many important things going on at work that I don't need to come home to all your negativity.

Obviously, that doesn't feel very good. It can either shut down communication or fuel an argument. This would be a good time to step back so you can begin to take the steps in what *you* can do to communicate better. It's a good time to put the Coherent Communication technique into practice. A good place to start—step 1 of the technique—might be to do Attitude Breathing (chapter 4) to get coherent. The list below gives you some ideas of a replacement attitude. You could also do Heart-Focused Breathing (chapter 1) or Quick Coherence (chapter 2) for step 1.

Negative Attitudes and Feelings	Positive Replacement Attitudes and Feelings
Angry/Upset	Breathe calm or neutral to cool down
Anxious	Breathe calm
Fearful	Breathe courage, peace, or calm
"I can't"	Breath "I can"
Impatient	Breathe patience
Judgmental	Breathe ease, tolerance, or compassion
Rebellious	Breathe respect or calm
Self-pity/Poor me	Breathe maturity, confidence, or strength
Shamed/Guilty	Breathe kindness, care, or compassion for yourself

Let's say that in the example above, you use Attitude Breathing (chapter 4) and breathe in the attitude of calm. Once you genuinely feel calmer, you can speak from your heart, which might sound something like this:

Teen: I know you have a lot going on at work and have had to work longer hours than usual, but I don't really feel I have a bad attitude. It's just that I found out that my best friend is moving and it's all happening very suddenly. We grew up together, and I know I'm going to miss her. I'm a little bit afraid, too, because I already feel empty. I don't have any other friends that I'm that close to. On top of that, we're learning some new stuff in math class that I don't understand, and we have a test this Friday.

We can't guarantee that your parent will change his or her own attitude, but you can feel good about speaking from your heart and making a sincere attempt to sort things out. Be patient with yourself and with others, too. Communication may have been a big issue for a long time, and it would be unrealistic to think it will all suddenly change. Keep working at it. You may start communicating better than many, or most, adults do!

Communicating with Other Adults

You have other adults in your life than just your parents. You have teachers, coaches, counselors, your boss at work, and likely others. Just because they have certain roles, such as being your teacher or boss, doesn't mean that good communication just happens. Everyone, including you, has to adjust to your growth and changes. That can cause adults some insecurity. In their own way, some adults are working on bettering themselves just like teens. It's not that any road, smooth or bumpy, won't get us where we want to go, but a smooth ride can save a lot of time and energy and simply feel better along the way, too. Good communication can smooth a lot of the bumps. The sooner there is a bridge in communication, the sooner everyone can have greater understanding, patience, and deep care.

You don't have to learn another strategy of how to communicate better with other adults in your life. Follow the guidelines as discussed in the section above. It's that simple—but again, it's not always easy to do when long-standing issues or emotions are flaring. It starts with stepping back and getting coherent so you can approach conversations with calm and confidence. Your ability to self-regulate how you respond in situations is a big step in becoming more mature. And because of that, you may find that you gain the respect of adults because you bring maturity to a conversation rather than reactivity.

Now let's take a look at some other people with whom you communicate a lot—your peers. Because poor communication with your peers can be a big contributor to your stress levels, it's important to find ways to communicate well with them.

Communicating with Peers

Communicating with peers seems like it should be pretty easy. But, in fact, it can be just as big a stressor as communicating with adults. One reason, as we've said, is the transformation that teens go through—from changes in their bodies to mood swings, tantrums, and unsettled emotions like anger and anxiety. Teens are also faced with pressure from their peers to experiment with risky behavior—everything from skateboarding down the railing of a big set of steps at the local library to taking drugs and having sex.

How teens digitally communicate with others also produces significant anxiety. With the explosion of social media and mobile phones, many of you are constantly dialed into your devices with your friends and "Facebook-like" sites. Social media then becomes the stage for venting anger, gossiping about others, and dissing kids you may not like. It's the stage for sexting, too. Using social media in those ways only fuels hostility and creates a lot of drama and stress. Social media can also be a huge expenditure of time and can take away from any real and meaningful conversations you could have with your parents or peers.

Let's look at something else now that can take good communication offline—something that is more than likely present every day in your life. It's very common and you're probably quite familiar with it. One word sums it up, or at least part of it: drama.

Drama

Got any in your life? No doubt you have plenty of drama around you and hear or use the term "drama" a lot. The *Online Slang Dictionary* defines drama as a "constant source of interpersonal conflict." You probably see people getting caught up in all sorts of conflicts or maybe even creating it by gossiping about other people and situations that they really don't know anything about. They pass on what they've heard and, along the way, exaggerate it, put it on social media, and talk about it as though it's the end of the world. You probably know some people who seem to dramatize everything. You know—the drama queens or kings. A drama queen tells the first person she sees, "My dog jumped on me as I was leaving for school and got dirt all over my brand-new pants. They're ruined, and I look awful, and what are people going to think? I mean, look at my pants. See that dirty paw mark. Stupid dog. I can't believe he did that."

Even if you're not a drama queen or king, it doesn't mean you're drama free. As it turns out, drama doesn't just happen on the outside, although that's where it often plays out. Drama, in fact, starts on the *inside* and can have a big impact on how you communicate and relate to people. Typically, drama starts small, but then it gets pumped up and spreads quickly. Everything gets blown out of proportion, whether it is a put-down you believe someone gave you, something bad that might happen in your life, or relationship gossip.

Drama seems to be everywhere, but does it ever help find a good, reasonable solution to a situation? Of course it doesn't. In fact, meddling with drama usually only feeds it and makes a situation worse. Getting caught in the drama loop also wastes a ton of time.

Now let's look at the two levels of drama, which we think you'll find helpful in seeing what's really going on. The second level of drama in particular is one that might be new to you.

"At my school, there is a lot of drama! Little things become really big things. Soon the whole school knows. So I have to be really careful of what I say and to whom I talk about things. To be honest, I am a little paranoid."

Two Levels of Drama

Drama actually happens on two levels. One level is the drama that occurs after something has happened. For example, let's say one of your teachers got on your case for not having your homework finished. After she was finished talking with you, you felt scolded. Immediately, you found a couple of friends to tell them all about it and how unfair it was. You justify it by saying that this teacher is always on your case. You may even try to get them to take your side. A little later, you look for someone to listen to your story. Each time, the story gets bigger and bigger and more dramatic. A little bump becomes a hill, then a mountain. The result? A lot of stress for you.

Think of times you've gotten caught up in drama. It might not even be your own, but you find yourself getting sucked into someone else's drama about something that happened. Write these situations in your notebook. Doing so might help you think of even more. Then ask yourself if getting caught up in drama helped at all, or if you ended up feeling like you were spinning your tires in a drama rut.

What effect did all that complaining and rehashing the story with your friends have on finding a solution to the issue? Whose energy are you draining when you tell that story over and over? That's just one level of drama, however.

The second level of drama is one that can sneak up on you without you even knowing it. This level of drama is all the inner drama, or inner "self-talk," that you have with yourself about the situation. You might think of it as complaining to yourself and rehashing what just happened. Hey, that's handy when there's no one around to listen, but in the end it only makes matters worse and keeps you on the drama treadmill going nowhere fast.

Inner drama is all the blaming, replaying, worrying, or justifying of your perspective after a drama-filled situation or event—perhaps something like this: *My friends always get to go out on school nights, and it's so unfair that my parents only let me hang out with my friends on the weekends.* Or, *Why did so-and-so avoid eye contact or barely look at me today? Doesn't she like me anymore?* You tell yourself a story that may not be entirely true. And the more replaying you do—some teens blame others, while others judge themselves—the bigger you make the issue and the bigger the energy drain becomes. The inner grumbling or worrying keeps the issue alive, and before you know it, you're off telling someone else about what happened. It might even land on your social media page.

All of this rehashing of feelings and complaining about a situation rarely leads to a resolution of the actual or perceived issue. More than likely, it only makes it worse. No wonder drama stresses you out.

Taking charge of the drama in your life begins with getting to the source of the drama. The first step in putting the brakes on drama, either your own or someone else's, is to become aware when you are getting caught up in it. If you don't acknowledge it, you can't possibly do anything about it. Sometimes listening for drama in another person can help you see it. Taking on drama and reducing it, then, is an inside job. Instead of feeding drama, starve it!

As you've been reading, you may already have thought of times you've gotten caught up in drama or maybe created some yourself. Make note of these and write them in your notebook. Be on the lookout for drama throughout an entire day and see how much drama plays out both around you and inside you. For instance, you might overhear someone at lunch talking about how unfair it is that his parents grounded him just because he wasn't following some of the house rules of keeping his room clean and cleaning the kitchen thoroughly once a week. You hear him give all the reasons that he's upset about being grounded. The story goes on and on, and the friend who is listening adds to it by agreeing that it's totally unfair. Then someone else joins them, and it's almost as though they try to outdo each other with who has the biggest complaint. This is why it's so important to first recognize when drama happens so you can do something about it.

What to Do When Drama Engulfs You

One way to become more aware of your outer and inner drama is to ask yourself in any situation or conversation, *Which quadrant of the Landscape am I in right now?* Be really honest with yourself. When you are in either of the left two quadrants, it can be a sign that drama is lurking. That's because any of the emotions on the left side of the Landscape (chapter 3) can be fuel for drama. After all, you probably wouldn't be complaining and worrying about something someone did or said if you weren't angry, frustrated, anxious, or fearful about it. Negative emotions can drive drama in a very big way.

Once you notice you are on the left side of the Landscape and see that you are fueling the drama, you can take charge and stop the drama in its tracks. Ask yourself, *What technique can I do right now that will help me stop fueling the drama and that will stop the energy drain?* You now know techniques that can help you shift on the spot to the right side of the Landscape or at least reduce the drama down to a manageable level. You could choose any of them: Heart-Focused Breathing (chapter 1), Quick Coherence (chapter 2), or Attitude Breathing (chapter 4). Or you might do Freeze Frame (chapter 5) to get insight into a more appropriate response. And be sure to put the Coherent

Communication technique that you learned in this chapter to use. See for yourself what a difference it can make for you. When you get drama out, you can see the situation in a more mature way. You might find the situation was really not that big of a deal after all. And even if it was, you've gotten yourself into a better place to work it out.

***

We've talked about many aspects of communication and some of the challenges that we all encounter. Paying closer attention to your role in any communication is important if you want to get along better with people and have less drama in your life. Learning how to communicate better now will not only help you be more responsible and bring more maturity to life's inter-actions, but you'll also build a good foundation for communi-cating your best throughout your life. So keep practicing! It will pay off for building better relationships, which we'll talk about in the next chapter.

Your Stress-Bustin', Resilience-Boostin', On-the-Go Action Plan

1. Identify three times each day when you will practice the Coherent Communication technique. Do this for the next few days.

2. To avoid drama, practice the Coherent Communication tech-nique before sending a text message or an e-mail, or when you're at school hanging out with your friends.

3. Write down in your notebook how communicating from the right side of the Emotional Landscape (chapter 3) affects your conversations.

4. Practice being on the lookout for drama. Remember, it's really easy to get pulled into it, so when you see it, put on the brakes by practicing any of the techniques you've learned so far.

5. Continue to use the Emotional Landscape (chapter 3) to identify energy-depleting and energy-renewing emotions. Use the techniques to stop the drain and shift to the right side of the Landscape. When you do shift to the right side, what do you notice or observe about yourself? Do you feel better? Can you think more clearly? Write your observations down in your notebook.

chapter 8

Relationships
Building Deeper Connections

Relationships are an important part of our lives. Our relationships can make life more enjoyable. They also can give us a boost and help us feel supported and encouraged when we're feeling down. If your best friend moves out of town, you might feel lonely and sad. Your mom or dad, noticing that, might sit and talk with you while you vent or cry about the loneliness you feel. Sitting and talking won't change the fact that your best friend moved, but having someone there just to listen can help you feel like you're not alone.

On the other hand, relationships can also be the source of a lot of stress. Have you ever thought about the amount of stress you accumulate from your relationships with friends, classmates, family, or teachers? As you've learned in this book, when you're feeling stressed, you probably aren't bringing your very best to your relationships or to anything you do. Feeling stressed can rob you of real connection with people, and it can also rob you of personal fulfillment. Feeling stressed can make it difficult to be a supportive friend for someone having a tough time. It can also affect your schoolwork, how well you play in the next ball game, and the quality of your relationships—all of them.

Interesting research has shown that the quality of our relationships can affect how we see life's situations. To illustrate the study's findings, imagine someone standing at the bottom of a hill with an empty backpack on his back. He sees the hill as having a certain incline or steepness. When rocks are put into his backpack, the hill looks steeper, even without taking a single step forward. Likewise, the "weight" of the accumulated stress we carry, like the weight of the rocks in the backpack, affects how we see everyday situations. Issues and situations may look bigger than they really are.

The study also found that when a friend stands next to the person with the backpack full of rocks, the hill does not seem as steep. Not only that, but the longer the two people have been friends, the less steep the hill seems! This suggests that our interactions and connections with other people do in fact have a real impact on us and literally how we perceive the world. This means that the quality of our relationships, without our even knowing it, affects how easy or hard life seems.

Below are some strategies you can use to improve the quality of your relationships as well as increase resilience in your relationships. Resilience in relationships means being flexible and adaptable in your relationships. Your personality, background, current circumstance, and, perhaps more than anything else, your level of comfort with the strategies we'll outline next will determine which ones you choose to use. But even putting a couple of them into practice can make a big difference. If you combine some of these new strategies with the skills from chapter 7, Coherent Communication—deep heart listening and speaking from your heart—and Attitude Breathing from chapter 4, you are well on your way to developing an

intelligent skill set that can help create better relationships—a
skill set that you can use for a lifetime.

Speaking from Your Heart

In any relationship, whether it is with a family member, a
friend, a teacher, or a boyfriend or girlfriend, speaking from
your heart can help build a stronger and deeper connection.
Speaking from your heart means honestly acknowledging what
you are feeling or thinking, first with yourself and then with
the other person. That might seem difficult at first because most
people have not learned to be really honest with themselves
and others. Additionally, the mind thinks that being honest
about how you really feel is risky, and it may even create more
pain or cause more confusion and tension. That sometimes is
the case. However, by being honest with yourself and acknowledging your deeper feelings, you open the door for finding
positive solutions to challenges in the relationship. Speaking
from your heart really means bringing a more mature attitude
and approach to building better relationships built on trust and
honesty. That maturity can help you know what is appropriate to share with someone rather than dumping your internal
drama on them. It is a way of being true to yourself and another
person so that your feelings, attitudes, and perceptions are
understood—or at least shared. It helps you to share your real
feelings, which can enhance your communication and connection with someone. So, how do you develop the ability to speak
from your heart?

When you face a challenge in a relationship, first acknowledge your feelings and how you see the situation. You might

feel hurt by what someone said or did, and you might say, "I am angry. I don't want to be around you." The normal thing would be to blame that person, let the tension build, and share negative comments with friends or peers behind the other person's back. That, however, builds a wall of separation. You both suffer as a result. When you face a challenge like this, take a moment and get coherent by practicing one of the techniques you've learned. You may find that you can give the person the benefit of the doubt. Or your intuition might give you clarity of a more mature way to respond, such as "I am still having difficulty from our last conversation. I feel misunderstood. Can we try again?" In many cases, the other person may have had a bad day when she made her comment, or maybe you misinterpreted her behavior. That happens a lot. Being honest and acknowledging your hurt can help ground you. Going deeper into your heart allows your intuition to surface and show you other ways to approach a situation. In a case like this, you may find it helpful to use a technique such as Attitude Breathing (chapter 4). Deep heart listening (chapter 7) also can open you up so you can hear the essence or deeper meaning of what the other person is saying, which can help your relationship grow stronger.

Although it's not always easy to speak from your heart, your relationships will be built on a stronger foundation if you are genuine with another person. Again, sharing what you are thinking and feeling with another person doesn't mean that you blurt out everything that's on your mind in that moment. It means discerning the appropriate thing to say and the appropriate time to say it with a genuine attitude. Doing so will pay dividends for the rest of your life.

Develop Compassion for Yourself and Others

Being genuine with how you really feel inside can be a valuable practice because it can help build trust in relationships. Another practice is developing compassion for yourself and for others. *Compassion* is having care for, sensitivity to, and kindness to someone—even yourself—who is having a hard or challenging time.

Why is compassion important? To relieve stress in yourself and to have better relationships, it's very important to be patient with and have compassion for others who are experiencing a lot of stress. There can't be real relief from stress for one person or a group of people if someone is still upset and stewing about something. That only keeps alive the endless cycles of stress, anger, and disconnect between people. Blaming others is the easiest thing to do when we get upset. Most of the time people don't have a clue what others are really feeling or how their actions affect others. A lot of people's emotional difficulties come from not knowing how to handle their emotions that may get triggered in different situations, so they stay upset and that creates more stress.

When you find yourself in a situation like this, be as easy on yourself as you can. Have compassion for yourself. Compassion can help you ease up on yourself so you feel more balanced. It can help you build a sense of inner security where you are more comfortable and confident being in your own skin. Have compassion for other people, too. In doing so, you might come to see that they, like you, are doing the best they can right now. There may be some situations that are really difficult, and you may feel like fear or anger is bottled up inside you. Do a Heart Lock-In (chapter 6) and send compassion to yourself, the other person, and even the situation itself. Or breathe in compassion as you do Attitude Breathing (chapter 4). Remember, too, that emotions and their intensity change over time. Sometimes when feelings are the most intense, it can be good to go for a long walk, listen to some favorite music, or even dance. Practicing Heart-Focused Breathing (chapter 1) can be helpful, too. Before talking with the person with whom you're having difficulties, perhaps you can share your situation with a trusted friend or adult. Or practice Freeze Frame (chapter 5) so you get clearer inside yourself about what you might say or do.

Having compassion for someone and a feeling of genuine care when they are upset or made fun of by their peers might feel a little uncomfortable for you. But situations like that actually can bring out the best in you. If you feel tension in the air or see that someone is really upset or bothered by something, go to your heart and practice Attitude Breathing (chapter 4), breathing in compassion and understanding. It can help relieve the tension you feel and might just help the other person, too.

By developing more compassion, you not only reduce stress that can fuel situations, but you're also bringing more maturity to the situation. Having compassion also can foster more trust and a deeper connection between people.

Avoid Judgments

One of the biggest causes of conflict in relationships is the judgments we form about a person or situation, and often our judgments are negative—she's stupid, he's fat, or my parents are so unfair. The tricky thing with a judgment is that it is not necessarily true, and even if it is, we can create a lot of drama around it and put a lot of energy into it. Often you may not even know that you're judging someone. You say, "Well, of course, he is an idiot. Isn't it obvious?" If you make a lot of negative judgments, it can become a habit and you're likely to see everything—and everyone—through a judgmental lens. Judging then becomes the normal way you see things. The mind forms negative judgments when it's going too fast. Getting coherent, then, can slow down the mind so you get a more balanced perspective.

It's easy to disguise judgments. After all, it seems like you're just making an observation that someone is "stupid," "ugly," "a loser," "a dumb jock," "clueless," and the list goes on. Their behavior matches your observations. Often, though, and this is important, *you* may have an emotional charge—such as irritation, disgust, anger, or fear—that is connected to the person or issue that fuels the judgment. If someone judges *you*, however, that's a whole different story! It doesn't feel good and it's clear to you that they are wrong.

"Our health education teacher gave us an assignment. We were supposed to practice Heart-Focused Breathing while walking across campus and try not to judge anyone. She wanted us to celebrate how unique everyone is and not how they are different from us. That was really fun to appreciate people rather than judge them."

So begin to notice when you slip into judging others. Keep in mind that more than likely you may have done the very thing that you're judging them about. When you do find yourself judging, practice Attitude Breathing (chapter 4) and breathe patience or an attitude of "maybe I don't really know what's going on with the other person." That can help bring you back into more balance.

Genuinely think about the importance of being more open-minded or tolerant before you judge someone. Isn't that what you want for yourself? In reality, it is *not* intelligent to judge people or issues or anything for that matter. Judging is the opposite of allowing people to be. Your true nature is to live your own life the very best you can and allow others to do the same. That's a great thing you can do for yourself and for the people you might be tempted to judge. You'll have less stress. When you have less stress, you're more resilient and can bring the best you to your relationships. Now let's look at something else that commonly gets in the way of our connection with other people—histories.

> "The social life in my school is crazy. We have all these different groups and everyone is judging each other all the time. But underneath the labels that everyone gives each other are real people who are pretty much the same as everyone else."

Handle Histories with Care

Histories are things that happened in the past that stack up and can have a huge effect on our current relationships. To understand what we mean by histories, we'll use the example that your brother tends to do certain things that upset you—like never walking or feeding the family dog, which is part of his responsibility. He rarely cleans up the bathroom you share, and he leaves his clothes and wet towel on the floor. Your frustration builds up inside, and at some point, you explode with anger. Or maybe you had an argument with another girl a year ago about a boy you both liked. The anger you felt then still affects the conversations you have with her now.

Begin to notice if you have histories with people that affect how you relate with them today. If you discover that you do, practice one of the techniques you've learned in this book so that what has happened in the past in relationships doesn't cloud them now and in the future. You might start with Freeze Frame (chapter 5) and see what insight or solution your heart might have in store to help you with the situation. You might do Attitude Breathing (chapter 4) and breathe in a "no big deal" attitude. This is you taking care of yourself first so you can be more balanced and calmer in this relationship.

Makeovers are another habit that we can form without even knowing that we're doing it that can cause problems in any of our relationships. We'll talk about them next.

Watch for Makeovers

Have you ever heard people say after an argument with a friend, "I'm okay, everything's fine," when in fact they were really only half okay? We call that a makeover. *Makeovers* are lingering and unresolved feelings that you still have after an argument or an interaction with someone where you felt a lot of stress. Lurking under makeovers are deeper feelings that people just can't seem to change or "get over." That means that not only did they drain their battery during the argument, for example, but those unre-solved feelings can continue to create a separation between the two of you.

When you tell someone "I'm okay" after a disagreement, but you're still feeling angry or upset, that's the time to acknowledge the separation that you really feel. Then practice a technique such as Attitude Breathing (chapter 4). Makeovers can really take a toll on your relationships if you don't notice them and put the brakes on them. If you are only half okay and still feel upset, how do you think it's going to go the next time you see your friend? Makeovers don't lead to better communication because your genuine feelings are swept under the rug.

Watch for makeovers. They are only temporary patches. When you notice one, practice Attitude Breathing (chapter 4) or perhaps Freeze Frame (chapter 5) so you can stop the drain, feel better, and see the situation for what it really is. Practice a technique until you feel more balanced and calm. Do it for yourself, but don't be surprised if others notice how calm you are!

Provide a Solid Foundation for Romantic Relationships

The romantic relationships that last are the ones in which you become real friends first, or at least along the way. The sweetheart phase is just that—a phase with freshness and romance. People love that high-powered emotional feeling, but it can also be a roller-coaster ride that leaves you wondering if it's really worth it. When you build the relationship out of true friendship, you put a solid foundation under romance.

A special relationship is always going to be full of challenges. It's how you respond to challenges that count.

Let's say two people who are in a romantic relationship with each other start to have concerns about each other's friendships with other people. At this point, many people argue and fight and decide that they don't love each other anymore, and they go their separate ways. How might the situation be different if each were to be more patient with each other, have more compassion, practice Coherent Communication (chapter 7), speak from their hearts, and listen with the intent to understand?

We talked about being friends first and how that friendship can be the foundation for a lasting relationship. Being compassionate, patient, and supportive while speaking and listening from the heart are practices you can use in any relationship to help foster trust and a deeper connection. Trust and deeper connection are the building blocks for a strong foundation for lasting relationships. Having compassion can also help to build a sense of security and ease the pressure of expectations you place on yourself and on others.

Soften Your Expectations

One of the biggest keys in gaining your own sense of security in relationships where you feel comfortable to be yourself—whether it's with a romantic partner, friends, parents, or anyone else—is learning to love and care for someone without expectations about what they do or don't do. By finding your own sense of security where you are more confident in yourself, life is more likely to give you what you really want and not what your mind thinks it wants. Inner security gives you the power to love or care about someone with or without that love or care coming back the way you might want.

Understanding and practicing things that we discussed in this chapter, such as having compassion, speaking from the heart, and putting the brakes on judgments can ease much stress. This allows us to bring our very best to our relationships. In the next chapter, we're going to introduce three important strategies that can help you build and sustain your resilience.

Your Stress-Bustin' Resilience-Boostin', On-the-Go Action Plan

1. Over the next two or three days, write down in your notebook each time you notice you are judging someone or something. Be very honest with yourself.

2. Also, make note of times in the last two or three days when you found yourself doing a makeover—where you said, for instance, that everything was okay when you really had unsettled feelings. Again, be very honest with yourself and don't let your head justify makeovers.

3. For one judgment you made and one makeover you noticed, do a Freeze Frame (chapter 5) to get clarity on how you might handle or approach each so you don't get stuck processing them over and over. See if you can find a different way of looking at each one. In doing so, you'll both relieve tension and stress and also build stronger relationships.

4. Practice Attitude Breathing (chapter 4) several times during the next week, breathing in an attitude of tolerance or compassion while interacting with your peers, friends, or family.

See if that practice helps you be more self-aware and caring toward others.

5. Pay attention to any histories you might have with friends, peers, or adults. Write them down in your notebook. Use Attitude Breathing to try to neutralize any past judgments or hurts and bring in more care and compassion to those relationships.

chapter 9

Three Key Strategies
Building and Sustaining Your Resilience

You've covered a lot of ground in this book. Congratulations for sticking with us in learning how to better handle all the day-to-day stuff! We know there are days when a lot comes at you, and we genuinely hope that practicing the techniques we've offered in this book is helping make a difference in your life. Keep at it! Remember, challenges will keep showing up. That's part of life. The important thing is that you can keep showing up with your heart. Put your heart to work for you again and again, and you'll find you can better handle the day-to-day stuff that comes up. You'll also feel more confident and calmer, and will have greater inner security.

You've been introduced to techniques designed to help reduce your stress by taking charge of the root cause of your stress—how you respond in situations. In this chapter, we're going to talk about three key strategies for not only building your resilience so you can better handle anything that comes up, but also for sustaining your resilience.

Practicing these three strategies—prep, shift and reset, and sustain—can help you more effectively regulate your energy and emotions throughout the day. That means making adjustments right on the spot by stopping energy leaks and recharging while you're on the go. These three key strategies serve as a guide for when to practice the techniques. Let's see how they work.

First Key Strategy: Prep

What do top athletes and musicians do before performing for thousands of people? They prep. They practice and charge up their inner battery to be at their best level to perform. Before any important activity or event, but especially before ones that are typically stressful like taking a big test, it makes sense to charge up your inner battery by practicing one of the techniques you have already learned—like Quick Coherence (chapter 2)—for two minutes.

To prep for something means to be ready for it in advance so you're better equipped and prepared to deal with it with more ease. When you study for a test, you are prepping for it. As you very well know, the outcome—that is, the grade you get on the test—will very likely be quite different if you don't study for the test. With a genuine effort to study, you feel more confident when you take the test. You may not necessarily ace the test, but you can be sure that you'll do better on it than if you hadn't prepared at all.

It isn't only tests you can prep for. You can prep for just about anything. If you're on a sports team, for example, each day that you practice, you are prepping. You do this so that, when the day of the big game comes, you and the team as a whole will be ready to meet that challenge. If you didn't practice, the outcome probably wouldn't be very pretty.

Maybe your family is planning a camping trip. To prep for it, you get out the tent and check to be sure it's waterproof and gather all the miscellaneous supplies. Don't forget the food! If you didn't prep for the camping trip, one rainy night you might find that the tent has some major leaks and all of your sleeping bags get soaked. Imagine the outcome of that—a tired, wet, miserable family!

For the purposes of our discussion of how to reduce stress, *prep* means to be emotionally prepared and balanced before an upcoming situation or event. If you think about it, there are likely events or recurring situations that typically cause you a lot of stress. They are different for everyone, but we all have them. It could be certain classes or teachers at school, or communications with parents or your peers, and so on. Why not prep yourself before you have to step into those situations or events? Prepping puts you on the right side of the Emotional Landscape (chapter 3), the side from which you have greater ability to be in charge of how you respond in a situation. You can maintain your composure better, think more clearly, and access your intuition more easily so you'll know how to handle things more wisely and effectively.

Again, we'll use the example of taking a test. Let's say you're anxious and nervous before taking your math test because you really want to do well, but the material you've been studying is pretty tough. Your nerves are off the charts! When you sit down to take the test, you feel like an emotional wreck. How well do you think you're going to do? You might even say to yourself, *I am so anxious that I can't think clearly! How can I possibly remember anything?* Recall from chapter 2 that emotions such as anxiety create an incoherent heart rhythm. That signals to the brain a "static message," and indeed, you literally can't think clearly or your mind "goes blank." It's just the way your body works. The outcome for that test, then, is you won't be able to do your best and you'll get a lower score.

But let's say you prep for that test—not just content-wise but emotionally as well. When you first notice that you're feeling anxious about the test, maybe even while you're eating breakfast, you practice one of the techniques to get coherent. Maybe you start by doing Heart-Focused Breathing (chapter 1) and as you continue doing it, you notice that you begin to feel calmer. Your mind might wander off and start thinking about the test again, but you remember to refocus your attention around your heart and you continue practicing it until you feel calm. That's prepping! You might decide it would be a good idea to keep doing Heart-Focused Breathing on the way to school and especially right before you walk in and sit down to take the test. Feeling calmer feels much better than feeling anxious, so that's one benefit. When you feel calmer, you can think better and probably will do better on the test, assuming you studied for it! By doing Heart-Focused Breathing, you also stopped the energy drain caused by anxiety that was sure to zap your inner battery. Let's see how fifteen-year-old Brandon deals with an important math test.

I got a really bad grade on my last math test, and I had to do well on the next one, which was coming up in a couple of days. I had just learned a couple of the techniques and decided to do Heart-Focused Breathing. I used it most of the time until the test, including when I walked down the hall, sat down to study, and all the rest of the day, too. I could feel myself getting and staying calm. That started to give me confidence that I wouldn't be really anxious and nervous when I was taking the test.

On the day of the test, I walked into the classroom and sat down at my desk and kept doing Heart-Focused Breathing. I didn't even open my notes. I just sat calmly and looked straight ahead. The other kids in the class were doing that last-minute cram thing, and some of them looked over at me and wondered what I was doing. My teacher did, too. He gave us the test, and I felt really good. A couple of times I got to a question that I wasn't sure of and I could feel myself getting anxious again, so I did some more Heart-Focused Breathing and it really helped. I got an 87 percent on the test, which was a huge relief. You can be sure that I will continue to practice Heart-Focused Breathing. It absolutely works!

Heart-Focused Breathing (chapter 1) is often the first technique people use because it's simple, and, as Brandon just said, it works. You could also do Quick Coherence (chapter 2) or Attitude Breathing (chapter 4).

The value of prepping cannot be overstated! Here are some times that you might prep:

* before you begin your day—getting coherent to set the tone for the day

* before you do homework or take a test

* before making decisions

* before a situation where you feel anxious or afraid

* before making a presentation

* before having an important talk with your parents, a teacher, or a friend

In addition to prepping in general, for which you may use any of the techniques you've learned so far, there's also a specific technique to use for prepping. Let's take a look at that now.

The Prep Technique

The prep technique can prevent a lot of stress and energy drain by helping you be more emotionally prepared for an upcoming situation or event that typically causes you stress or for which you want to perform your best. Olympic athletes, for example, know the value of prepping before an event because they know it can improve their performance. Perhaps you have seen them on TV trying to get into the "zone" minutes before an important event. They visualize just the right moves to make and especially imagine themselves staying composed if they make mistakes. They know and value the importance of staying calm, balanced, and focused to help prevent draining their energy. They want to stay clearheaded so they can perform at their very best.

A genuine commitment is key in making the prep technique effective. It's not merely a mental exercise, and it's not just thinking about being calm and balanced. It's about breathing in through the heart area to get coherent and then *imagining* staying calm, composed, and resilient *throughout* the event, situation, or interaction.

To help you learn how to use the prep technique, we'll first describe its three steps. Next, we'll give you the Quick Steps, which you can use to refresh your memory. Then, to help you get the most out of practicing the prep technique, we'll explain it step by step so you'll better understand the entire technique.

Technique: Prep Technique

Step 1: *Identify an upcoming event, situation, or interaction that you are concerned about.*

Step 2: *While doing Heart-Focused Breathing, see or imagine yourself in that event, situation, or interaction. With genuine feeling, visualize being calm, balanced, and resilient throughout.*

Step 3: *See yourself remembering to recenter in your heart and take charge of your feelings if you start to overreact or lose emotional composure.*

Prep Technique Quick Steps

1. *Do Heart-Focused Breathing.*

2. *Visualize remaining calm and composed.*

3. *See yourself recentering as needed.*

Step by Step: How to Do the Prep Technique

Step 1: Identify an upcoming event, situation, or interaction that you are concerned about.

Identify a situation where you can apply the prep technique. For example, going to the dentist may not be on your Favorite-Things-to-Do list, so it's a perfect situation where you can use the prep technique! (Other everyday situations where you need to prep might include facing a challenging conversation with someone, taking an important test, or participating in a big athletic event.)

Step 2: While doing Heart-Focused Breathing, see or imagine yourself in that event, situation, or interaction. With genuine feeling, visualize being calm, balanced, and resilient throughout.

Begin by doing Heart-Focused Breathing (chapter 1) and as you do it, imagine yourself walking (using our example from above) into the dentist's office and sitting in the chair. Now, visualize and *feel* yourself walking in, sitting in the chair, and feeling calm and balanced. Continue doing this until you genuinely feel calm and hang out in that feeling for two or three minutes—or longer! The longer you spend doing this, the more familiar that calm feeling becomes. Take your time and don't rush this step.

Step 3: See yourself remembering to recenter in your heart and take charge of your feelings if you start to overreact or lose emotional composure.

This step is very important, too. Visualize the dentist walking into the room. All of a sudden you feel anxious or maybe even afraid. Here's where you "take charge" and make a choice to shift back to focusing on your heart. Once again, visualize yourself feeling calm. Notice yourself making that shift and hold that calm feeling steady. Again, don't rush this. You might then visualize your dentist starting to work on your teeth and that you get anxious again. Shift and recenter in your heart again and continue doing Heart-Focused Breathing as you visualize and feel yourself *feeling* calm. While you still may have some butterflies in your stomach, you probably will notice that they are greatly reduced.

Practice the prep technique often and with sincerity before you go to the dentist or whatever situation you identify in step 1. When you actually are sitting in the dental chair and not just imagining being there, you may find you're already calmer. And if you should begin to feel a little anxious, you have already practiced recentering in your heart by doing Heart-Focused Breathing and imagining yourself *feeling* calm. You can do it again right there on the spot.

Practicing the Prep Technique Right Now

For the next three or four minutes, practice the prep technique. Choose a real situation where you think it would be helpful to use it. Take your time with it and see what you notice as you do it. Write down in your notebook the situation and your observations. Have fun giving it a try!

We talked earlier about prep as a key strategy to build resilience. The prep technique is certainly one you can use to be better prepared before any situation, so you may want to practice using different situations. You could use it, for example, if you've been in a difficult situation such as being bullied or harassed. Using the prep technique, visualize standing near the person who bullied you. *Feel* yourself standing with greater confidence and calm. Hold steady in that feeling. See yourself remembering to recenter if feelings of fear come in. It's a very good technique to use to help you handle difficult situations like this.

Second Key Strategy: Shift and Reset

Now let's look at the second key strategy, which is called *shift and reset*. The name accurately describes what to do—you *shift* back to calm and composure and *reset* into that balanced state (which can help you maintain your composure) after a stress reaction, large or small. It's a simple practice, but when you've been triggered and you're angry, for example, you will need to make an effort and an inner commitment to calm down. Shift and reset just as soon as you can remember to do so. The faster you can shift and reset, the more energy you'll save by stopping your stress response in its tracks.

Remember Brandon's story above? He prepped by practicing Heart-Focused Breathing (chapter 1) before he walked into the classroom and also as he sat at his desk before being handed the test, which helped him have more confidence going into the test. He said that when taking the test, some questions he was unsure of popped up, causing him to feel anxious. Right there on the spot, he did Heart-Focused Breathing to shift and reset back to feeling calm and more confident. If he had not shifted and reset, he likely would have continued to feel anxious and his anxiety may have gotten even worse. He recognized that he had a *choice* either to continue with the test while feeling anxious or to find his way back to feeling calm. He could have tried to answer the questions with a befuddled mind or with a mind that could think and reason clearly. That makes for very different results on the test.

When should you use the shift and reset strategy? Here are several times when you may find it helpful:

* ✱ when someone says something that upsets you

* ✱ when you're having a difficult time focusing and concentrating

* ✱ if you feel afraid

* ✱ if you're standing in a line and feel impatient or frustrated

* ✱ when you do something that is embarrassing

Heart-Focused Breathing (chapter 1) is a great technique to use to shift and reset. To reinforce and add more staying power, do Quick Coherence (chapter 2) or Attitude Breathing (chapter 4) until you genuinely feel a deeper sense of calm, composure, or confidence.

Shift and Reset in Difficult Situations

Some situations can really be upsetting or challenging. When you feel freaked out, frazzled, or frozen, an effective shift and reset on the spot can be difficult to accomplish. But that does not mean giving up. Do try to shift and reset, but instead of expecting to clear away the intense emotion, try to go to neutral. Neutral means you have not resolved the issue; you may feel wronged or too hurt to greatly weaken the powerful emotion, but instead you try to manage your behavior as best you can so you don't do or say something stupid. You are doing your best to hold it together. You may have gotten an intuitive insight and you decided to just chill out, knowing that the incident will pass. You will survive, but you need some time to regroup and regain your composure. That is having true compassion for yourself, which leads us to the third key.

Third Key Strategy: Sustain

To *sustain* means to hold steady. The goal is, once you're coherent and feeling more balanced, to try to hold steady so you're not bouncing emotionally all over the place. With practice, it can become a new way of life. It's like a surfer riding the waves with balance and ease. When a big emotional wave comes, you can better maintain your balance and make adjustments quickly rather than wiping out.

One way to look at sustain is the practice of the first two key strategies—prep, and shift and reset. You prep to get coherent so you're more balanced and composed before an upcoming event or conversation, and if you get annoyed or feel impatient, you shift and reset right on the spot so you can get back to a coherent, composed, and balanced place inside. Together those strategies will help you create and hold on to an inner steadiness.

There's another way you can think of sustain as a strategy. Let's say you're having a great day and you feel like you're in sync and are able to "go with the flow" with ease. That great feeling is worth sustaining and hanging on to! Take advantage of those "feel good" days and practice a technique such as Quick Coherence (chapter 2) to help sustain your steadiness.

When Will You Apply Sustain?

Practically speaking, using sustain means carving out several two- to four-minute blocks of time during the day when you can practice one of the techniques such as Heart-Focused Breathing (chapter 1) or Quick Coherence (chapter 2). Those times could include when you drive to school, walk across your school campus in between classes, wait for a class to begin, or hang out at the end of lunch or with a few friends. There is always time to practice one of the techniques we've discussed because you do them on the go. Using any of the techniques on a regular basis will help you have less stress and build more resilience in your system.

The Value of Prep, Shift and Reset, and Sustain

By using the key strategies of prep, shift and reset, and sustain to get coherent, you create and sustain more flow and balance throughout the day. The more you practice staying composed and balanced, the more resilience and energy reserves you will have to maintain your ability to flex and flow.

It takes making a genuine effort to sustain more coherence and to reduce the drain of energy-zapping emotions so you don't fall prey to feeling irritated, worried, or frustrated, being judgmental, having self-doubt, or blaming others. It's easy to rehash issues and get stuck in the same depleting feelings over and over, which reinforces those patterns in the brain. Responses then become automatic. You end up acting out before being able to think clearly. Most people don't realize their automatic responses have become unconscious habits. This is why it's so important to practice the techniques you've learned on a regular basis and to use the three key strategies—prep, shift and reset, and sustain—as your guide of when to use the techniques.

Here is a brief summary of the three key strategies:

* **Prep** to be more coherent, to set the tone for the day, and to be more composed before upcoming stressful events, such as taking a test or a having a difficult conversation.

* **Shift and reset** to a more coherent state as soon as possible after a stress reaction to minimize energy drains.

* **Sustain** your resilience throughout the day by regularly practicing the techniques on the go.

Using the three strategies of prep, shift and reset, and sustain as a guide of when to practice the techniques can produce a real change in your physiology over time. By doing so, you build resilience in your body as reflected by changes in your heart rhythms. Research by the HeartMath Institute confirms this.

The HeartMath Institute researchers led a large study in a high school. They wanted to see if there would be any measureable changes in the students' heart rhythms if the students practiced the techniques on a regular basis. The study took place over one semester, which was about four months. The students were taught the same techniques you've learned in this book, which they were encouraged to practice frequently. The school also had available technology that showed the students if they were in a coherent state or not. The technology was provided to help reinforce their practice of the technique.

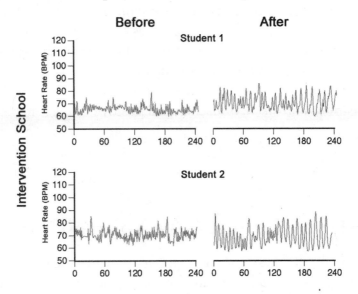

The graphs show examples of the heart rhythms of two of the students. One recording was taken for each student before they were taught the techniques. Those heart rhythms are shown in the two graphs on the left. After four months, the students' heart rhythms were measured again by the researchers. Those measurements are shown in the graphs on the right. What's important to note is that when the students' heart rhythms were measured the second time (after they had practiced the techniques for the semester), there is more *amplitude* or height in the right two graphs. In other words, the distance from the tops to the bottoms of the "wave" is a greater distance than those in the two graphs on the left. That means that physiologically the students had built more resilience into their systems.

If you look closely, you can also see that the patterns of the heart rhythms in the right two graphs are more coherent than those in the graphs on the left. Remember, the students were not practicing a technique when these measures were made. By practicing the techniques on a frequent basis, the students trained their nervous systems to be more coherent. This means that coherence became natural and more automatic.

Parents and teachers also noticed positive changes in behavior, such as students being more in control of their emotions and less reactive. Not only that, but they also had significantly higher test scores.

Lasting Change: Give Yourself Time

As you use the three key strategies and practice the techniques, allow yourself some time to iron out issues in which you've invested a lot of emotional energy. For example, you can't expect to transform a lifelong anxiety issue during the first five minutes you practice a technique. Over time, however, many people have seen genuine improvements from worry, fatigue, tension, frustration, and other stress symptoms after just a few days or a few weeks of practice. The more regularly you practice increasing and sustaining coherence, the sooner you will experience change, as the above graphs show.

All people have different things that cause them to feel stressed. What's important is not to compare yourself with others. After some practice, you may be surprised at how many situations or issues no longer get to you. Your life can become much smoother, even if some of the accumulated stress still hangs around despite your practice of the techniques.

Keep in mind that there won't be a total fix for everything that comes up. Life doesn't always serve up what we want, when we want it. When you face an especially sticky problem, go to your heart and apply a deeper care for all concerned, including yourself. Then you will be able to view the problem through a wider lens and more easily see what's best for everyone involved.

When things aren't changing as fast as you'd like, use Attitude Breathing (chapter 4) and breathe compassion for yourself and your challenges. That will help you to continue to move forward. Remember that you are building the power to respond thoughtfully and appropriately rather than automatically reacting, which in the long run will save you enormous amounts of energy and time.

Extra Power: Stay Genuine and Earnest

Very often, people's new self-improvement efforts fade once the initial high of enthusiasm and newness wears off. After all, it does take energy and effort to remember to practice the techniques. Progress can seem slow at times. You might even feel like you are going backward when you respond to a situation with an old reaction or emotional meltdown. Life happens. We are all works in progress. To keep yourself moving forward, stay genuine in your practice. *Genuine* means being sincere in putting the techniques into practice the very best that you can. Sometimes you may need to have an "I mean business" attitude to draw in more power to help you accomplish your goals.

Being genuine will bring you more insight so you can see things more clearly and can help you follow your heart's intuition and insights to keep you on track. When you have insight and a can-do attitude, you solve, resolve, and dissolve stress. You stop it in its tracks! You find a rhythm that takes you past many of the challenges you face. Life can become more enjoyable, too.

The Real You

In chapter 1, you did an exercise where you explored who you really are, what makes you come alive, and who you are when you're at your best. Go back to that exercise now and see if you've become a little more of who you really are as you've worked to transform the stress in your day-to-day life. For example, do you feel more confident or have more courage? Do you feel your fun side shines through more often and your true care comes through when you respond to someone who is down and out?

Maybe you discovered some other things about "your best you" along the way. Be sure to add any new discoveries to the list in your notebook or to your collage. Come back to the list of discoveries often to remind yourself of who you *truly* are, which comes from living from your heart.

What's Next?

You can go back through this book at any time, and we encourage you to do so. Hop from chapter to chapter for reminders of things you've explored with us. Read the techniques again—step by step—to refresh your mind on how to do them. Read the tips again, too. You may find that your understanding of techniques and the topics we've covered changes and deepens now that you've been practicing the techniques for a while.

Find different and creative ways to remind yourself to practice the techniques. Make a game out of plugging energy leaks and recharging your inner battery. Commit to meeting challenges with more calm and composure and see for yourself how that can benefit you and the situation. You might even create your own Stress-Bustin', Resilience-Boostin' On-the-Go Action Plan each week.

And last but not least, put your heart into it! Put your heart into everything you do. That's the key to transforming stress, to finding and being the *real you*.

Acknowledgments

The writing of *Transforming Stress for Teens: The HeartMath Solution for Staying Cool Under Pressure* is the result of many years of dedicated service by people helping others of all ages around the world to navigate today's fast-paced, stress-filled world with greater ease and inner composure. This book was made possible by the work of many people over many years who have worked with teens, and we simply do not have the space to acknowledge each one individually. Many of these people have worked tirelessly with children and teens in schools, counseling centers, youth organizations, and in families. Their experience has helped refine and improve the implementation of the HeartMath techniques over the years to make the practice of the HeartMath System as effective as possible for teens and youth. We are deeply grateful for their input and feedback, which is reflected in this book.

Special acknowledgment goes to Doc Childre, the founder of HeartMath. Without his vision and leadership, the techniques in this book and the research exploring the intelligence of our hearts would not exist. There are many people at HeartMath who have significantly contributed to the creation of the Heart-Math system to whom we are deeply grateful.

We would also like to thank Tesilya Hanauer and everyone at New Harbinger Publications for making this book possible. In particular, we'd like to thank our copy editor, Jean Blomquist, for her expertise in editing this book.

—Rollin McCraty, Jeff Goelitz, and Sarah Moor
HeartMath Institute

We at the Clemson University Youth Learning Institute appreciate the people of the HeartMath Institute for the work they have done for over two decades in developing a practical, science-based skill set that supports kids in classrooms and youth programs as well as supporting those teachers, coaches, and counselors who work with youth.

We also acknowledge the thousands of youth who have attended the programs provided by Clemson University's Youth Learning Institute where they learned to incorporate the Heart-Math skills into their lives. Many lives have been improved by the day-to-day practice of the HeartMath techniques.

—Stephen Lance
Youth Learning Institute
Clemson University

Rollin McCraty, PhD, is director of research at HeartMath® Institute Research Center. McCraty, a professor at Florida Atlantic University, is a psychophysiologist whose interests include the physiology of emotion. One of his primary areas of focus is the mechanisms by which emotions influence cognitive processes, behavior, and health. Findings from this research have been incorporated by HeartMath® in the development of simple, user-friendly mental and emotional self-regulation tools and techniques. People of all ages and cultures can use these tools and techniques *in the moment* to relieve stress and break through to greater levels of personal balance, stability, creativity, intuitive insight, and fulfillment. McCraty has written extensively and been widely published in his areas of scientific interest. He has been interviewed for many feature articles in publications that include *Prevention, Natural Health, Men's Fitness*, and *American Health* magazines. He has appeared in television segments for CNN Headline News, ABC World News Tonight, ABC's Good Morning America, NBC's Today Show, PBS's Body & Soul, and the Discovery Channel. In addition, he has been featured in many documentary films, including *I Am, The Truth, The Joy of Sox, The Power of the Heart, Solar Revolution*, and *The Living Matrix*, among others.

Sarah Moor is a HeartMath® master trainer and mentor. She is the instructor for HeartMath®'s coach/mentor certification training, assists in program design and development, and coordinates and mentors special HeartMath® projects. She has mentored thousands of individuals in learning how to incorporate the HeartMath® System into their daily lives.

Jeff Goelitz is currently program developer, senior trainer, and education specialist with the nonprofit HeartMath® Institute. He regularly consults with education professionals, mental health specialists, and parents around the United States and Canada to help improve the well-being of youth, parent/child communication, and classroom climate and performance. In the last fifteen years, he has created and contributed to numerous educational curricula and programs designed to improve social and emotional learning, including *The College De-Stress Handbook*.

Stephen W. Lance, MS, has over twenty years of experience in the field of youth development. Lance serves as executive director of Clemson University's Youth Learning Institute, which serves over 25,000 youth annually in diverse programs ranging from innovative schools, group homes, camping programs, and academic field study experiences.

Foreword writer **Steve Sawyer, LCSW, CSAC**, is clinical director and cofounder of New Vision Wilderness Therapy. He is a dual-licensed clinical social worker and certified substance abuse counselor, and a nationally recognized trainer in somatic trigger release techniques, Brainspotting, traumatic memory reprocessing, and HeartMath®.

More Instant Help Books for Teens

An Imprint of New Harbinger Publications

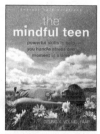

THE MINDFUL TEEN
Powerful Skills to Help
You Handle Stress One
Moment at a Time
ISBN: 978-1626250802 / US $16.95

**THE STRESS
REDUCTION WORKBOOK
FOR TEENS**
Mindfulness Skills to Help
You Deal with Stress
ISBN: 978-1572246973 / US $15.95

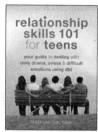

**RELATIONSHIP SKILLS
101 FOR TEENS**
Your Guide to Dealing with
Daily Drama, Stress &
Difficult Emotions Using DBT
ISBN: 978-1626250529 / US $16.95

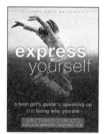

EXPRESS YOURSELF
A Teen Girl's Guide to Speaking
Up & Being Who You Are
ISBN: 978-1626251489 / US $16.95

**THE ANXIETY SURVIVAL
GUIDE FOR TEENS**
CBT Skills to Overcome
Fear, Worry & Panic
ISBN: 978-1626252431 / US $16.95

SELF-ESTEEM FOR TEENS
Six Principles for Creating
the Life You Want
ISBN: 978-1626254190 / US $16.95

newharbingerpublications
1-800-748-6273 / newharbinger.com
(VISA, MC, AMEX / prices subject to change without notice)

Follow Us

Don't miss out on new books in the subjects that interest you.
Sign up for our **Book Alerts** at **newharbinger.com/bookalerts**

Register your **new harbinger** titles for additional benefits!

When you register your **new harbinger** title—purchased in any format, from any source—you get access to benefits like the following:

- Downloadable accessories like printable worksheets and extra content
- Instructional videos and audio files
- Information about updates, corrections, and new editions

Not every title has accessories, but we're adding new material all the time.

Access free accessories in 3 easy steps:

1. Sign in at NewHarbinger.com (or **register** to create an account).

2. Click on **register a book**. Search for your title and click the **register** button when it appears.

3. Click on the **book cover or title** to go to its details page. Click on **accessories** to view and access files.

That's all there is to it!

If you need help, visit:

NewHarbinger.com/accessories

new harbinger
CELEBRATING
40 YEARS